Not So Obvious

An Introduction to Patent Law and Strategy

Second Edition

By Jeffrey Schox, Esq.

This book includes legal information, which is different than legal advice. If you need legal advice, you should engage in an attorney–client relationship with an attorney. Merely reading this book does not create such a relationship. While Jeffrey Schox has founded his own law firm (Schox PLC), the opinions in this book are his own and may not reflect the opinions of his firm or his clients.

Second Edition (September 2012)

Chapter Contents

6. Does the Invention Infringe Any Patents?

- Introduction
- Infringement Analysis
- Infringement Under the Doctrine of Equivalents
- Infringement Through Other Actions
- Defenses
- Remedies
- How to Design Around Problematic Patents

7. Who Owns the Patent Application?

- Who Is an Inventor?
- Who Is the Owner?
- Comparison of Assignments and Licenses

Special Thanks to

Jessica Hudak for her contributions, Lauren Koueiter for the cover design, and Jennifer Paine for her edits.

Additional Thanks to

My wife, Kate Schox, my friends John Manoogian III, Sam Valenti IV, Reilly Brennan, and Maria Walcutt, and to all of my past students for their encouragement and support.

Chapter One

Introduction to Intellectual Property

"Before [the adoption of the U.S. Constitution], any man might instantly use what another had invented; so that the inventor had no special advantage from his own invention. The patent system changed this ... and thereby added the *fuel of interest* to the *fire of genius*, in the discovery and production of new and useful things."— Abraham Lincoln

Chapter Contents

- What Is Intellectual Property?
    - Introduction
    - Patent Law
    - Trade Secret Law
    - Copyright Law
    - Trademark Law
    - Comparison of the IP Rights
- Why Do Societies Provide IP Rights?
    - A Brief History of Intellectual Property
    - Economic Incentive Theory
    - U.S. History of Patent Law
    - Letter from Thomas Jefferson Regarding Ideas
    - Contract Theory
- How Can You Leverage Intellectual Property?
    - Introduction
    - Protecting a Competitive Advantage
    - Generating Licensing Revenue from a Non-Competitor
    - Accessing the Channels or Assets of a Competitor
    - Deterring a Patent Infringement Lawsuit
    - Stimulating an Acquisition or Investment
    - Providing Leverage in a Negotiation with a Partner
    - Preventing Others from Patenting the Technology
    - Advertising Technical and Creative Ability and Increasing Credibility

What Is Intellectual Property?

Introduction

Intellectual property (also known as "IP") is an umbrella term for the legal rights that attach to inventions, confidential information, artistic expressions, and brands. The umbrella includes patent law, trade secret law, copyright law, and trademark law. The term "property" in intellectual property designates ownership and legal protection, like that of regular property (e.g., a house or a car). However, IP focuses on the products of the mind, rather than physical objects.

Although nearly every country in the world has enacted IP laws, "worldwide" rights (such as a worldwide patent) do not exist. Intellectual property laws are territorial; other than a few exceptions, IP laws do not extend beyond the border of an individual country or region. The discussion of this book will focus on the IP laws of the United States. In some sections, the discussion contrasts the IP laws of the United States with the IP laws of other countries.

Patent Law

In the United States, the patent laws are provided by the Constitution and are enacted by the federal government. A patent is the right to exclude others from making, using, or selling a particular *invention*. According to the United States Patent Statutes, any "process, machine, manufacture, or composition of matter" may be the subject matter of a patentable invention. Essentially anything but nebulous concepts and natural laws may be the subject matter of a patentable invention. The actual test for patentability imposes the following requirements: (1) the invention must be useful; (2) the invention must be novel; and (3) the invention must not be obvious to a person having ordinary skill in the art. Patents are not limited to pioneering advances that introduce new technologies; incremental steps that improve an existing technology may also be patentable.

There are three main kinds of patents:
- Utility patents, which are the most common, cover any "process, machine, manufacture, or composition of matter";
- Design patents cover the ornamental or aesthetic features of a product (e.g., an article of clothing or the exterior of a vehicle); and
- Plant patents cover asexually reproduced plants; such plants are reproduced by means other than from seeds (e.g., by the rooting of cuttings, by layering, or by grafting).

Patents are granted for a limited term. After this term expires, the subject matter of the patent enters the public domain and can be freely made, used, and sold. A utility patent filed on or after June 8, 1995, expires 20 years after the earliest *priority* date. (This date could be the filing date of the patent application, a "parent" patent application filed in the United States, or a "worldwide" PCT patent application.) A utility patent that was filed before June 8, 1995, expires either 17 years after the *issuance* date or 20 years after the *filing* date, whichever provides the longer term.

Patents, like all other intellectual property laws, are territorial. Suppose a United States patent application on an invention was filed, but no foreign patent applications were filed. Making, using, or selling the invention in foreign countries would not infringe the United States patent (unless the product was imported into the United States). Thus, to prevent the making, using, and selling of an invention in a particular country, a patent must be pursued in that country. To simplify the process, the inventor or applicant may file a so-called "worldwide" patent application under the rules of the Patent Cooperation Treaty (PCT). The PCT is an international process that facilitates filing patent applications in multiple countries; however, the PCT does *not* result in a single issued international patent. There are plans to establish an international patent in the future, but such a patent does not currently exist.

Comment on Patent Rights

Although a patent includes the right to exclude others, the patent does *not* include the right to actually make, use, or sell the invention. This concept will be explored in great detail in subsequent chapters; it is *the* most misunderstood concept in patent law. For now, imagine a first inventor who holds an early patent on a pioneering invention (e.g., Edison's light bulb), and a second inventor who holds a later patent on an improvement of the pioneering invention (e.g., Pipkin's frosted light bulb). The first inventor can prevent the second inventor from making, using, and selling the pioneering invention. On the other hand, the second inventor can prevent the first inventor from making, using, and selling the pioneering invention with the improvement. In fact, during an overlapping portion of the terms of the two patents, neither of the two inventors can make, use, or sell the pioneering invention with the improvement. In this situation, one of the inventors will typically license or sell his patent to the other (or the two inventors might cross-license their patent to each other).

Trade Secret Law

Trade secret laws are enacted by individual states—not by the federal government. While the laws of each state are fairly similar, the exact nature and protection of trade secret law varies from state to state. In most states, a trade secret is the right to prevent others from sharing *confidential information* that: (1) is economically valuable; (2) is neither known to others nor readily ascertainable; and (3) is maintained as a secret. Trade secrets do not have to satisfy the strict requirements of a patent. Therefore, they can include both technical and business information. Examples of information that may be protected by trade secrets include databases, customer lists, and manufacturing techniques.

To obtain legal protection, trade secrets should be identified and documented. Holders of trade secrets should be vigilantly policed for any violations of the trade secret. There is no "Trade Secret Office" or requirement to register a trade secret. (After all, the main requirement of a trade secret is that the information remains secret.) A holder of a trade secret must, however, indicate that the information is a trade secret; for example, the holder of the trade secret could mark the items "CONFIDENTIAL."

If a trade secret is properly maintained, it will endure forever (e.g., the Coca-Cola formula). If the trade secret is disclosed to the public, or if another person or company independently creates the same information, the protection on the trade secret is lost. Strangely, the person or company that independently created the same information may be able to subsequently protect their independent creation through patents, trade secrets, and/or copyrights. This quirk encourages the dissemination of the information through the patent system, but–after the patent term expires–it releases the invention into the public domain.

Copyright Law
Like Patent law, Copyright law is provided by the Constitution and enacted by the federal government. A copyright is the right to prevent the reproduction, the distribution, and the creation of derivative works of any original *artistic expression* fixed in a tangible medium (e.g., a piece of paper, a vinyl record, or a memory chip). Copyrights do not protect the underlying idea—only the *expression* of the idea. For example, a copyright on a system manual offers the right to prevent others from photocopying and distributing copies of the manual. However, it does not offer the right to prevent others from making or using the system described in the manual, or from writing a manual on

the system in his or her own words. To enforce a copyright, a company must prove that the alleged infringer had access to the original work and that the alleged copy is substantially similar to the original work. In other words, the copyright holder must prove that the infringer *copied* the original work.

Original works of artistic expression are *instantly* and *automatically* offered copyright protection upon the creation of the work. The enforcement of a copyright, however, must be preceded by a registration of the copyright in the United States Copyright Office. Copyright notices (e.g., "© Jeffrey Schox 2011") are inserted to notify others of an underlying copyright. As a general rule, for works created after January 1, 1978, copyright protection lasts for the life of the author plus an additional 70 years. For an anonymous work, a pseudonymous work, or a work made for hire, the copyright endures for a term of 95 years from the year of its first publication or a term of 120 years from the year of its creation, whichever expires first.

Comment on computer software

A *copyright* on computer software provides inexpensive IP protection against software pirates who make and sell *exact copies* of the computer software. A *patent* on the computer software provides expensive IP protection against competing products that incorporate the *inventions* of the computer software.

Trademark Law

Although not provided by the Constitution, trademark law is enacted by the federal government. Unlike the Patent and Copyright laws, however, Trademark law is *also* enacted by the states. One could receive a state trademark registration that provides protection within that state, as well as a federal trademark registration that provides protection throughout the United States.

A trademark is a word, symbol, color, musical phrase, or other *indicator* of the origin of particular goods or services. A trademark registered with the U.S. Patent and Trademark Office offers the right to exclude others in the United States from adopting and using a confusingly similar mark for similar goods or services. A trademark does not offer the right to exclude others from selling the same goods under an unrelated mark; in many situations, a trademark does not offer the right to exclude others from selling completely unrelated goods under the same mark. (For example, there is no confusion regarding the independent use of Cadillac for automobiles and Cadillac for cat food.)

Trademarks function to associate a particular product or service with a particular reputation or quality. In this manner, trademarks focus consumers' time and money on the goods and services that have proven their quality and/or value. The consumer may not know the actual manufacturer of the goods and services. Regardless of the actual source, trademarks identify and indicate to a consumer products or services as originating from a trusted source.

Comparison of Intellectual Property Rights

	Patents	Trade Secrets	Copyrights	Trademarks
Subject Matter	"Everything under the sun produced by man"	Business-related information (techniques)	Art, in an all-encompassing sense	Marks that identify the source of goods or services
Requirements	Utility, novelty, and unobviousness	Commercial value, generally not known, and reasonable efforts of secrecy	Originality, authorship, and fixation in a tangible medium	Use in commerce and either distinctiveness or secondary meaning
Protection Against Unathorized...	Making, selling, using, offering for sale, and importing	Stealing	Copies, performances, displays, and derivative works	Use of a mark that causes a likelihood of confusion
Endures Until...	20 years from the earliest priority date	Publicly disclosed	The life of the author + 70 years	Abandoned
Rights of Independent Creators	None	Full	Full	None
Estimated Costs	~$25,000	Security and confidentiality procedures	~$250	~$2,500

Why Do Societies Provide IP Rights?

A Brief History of Intellectual Property Rights

Although intellectual property has become an increasingly important business asset, the actual concept of intellectual property is thousands of years old. Sybaris, a Greek colony in

Southern Italy about 800 BCE, may have enacted the first patent system. Many centuries later, the Greek writer Athenaeus stated, "The Sybarites ... made a law that ... if any confectioner or cook invented any peculiar and excellent dish, no other artist was allowed to make this for a year; ... in order that others might be induced to labour at excelling in such pursuits...." Athenaeus: The Deipnosophists – Book 12, Page 521 *Translated by C.D. Yonge* (1854).

In 1474, Venice enacted a law that "[E]very person who shall build any new and ingenious device ... not previously made in this Commonwealth, shall give notice of it to the office ... when it has been reduced to perfection so that it can be used and operated. It being forbidden to every other person in any of our territories ... to make any further device conforming with and similar to said [device]... for the term of 10 years" Venetian Patent Statute of 1474. Venice issued 1,600 patents in the 110 years between 1490 and 1600 AD. Of these 1,600 patents, Venice issued a patent to Galileo in 1594 for his "machine for raising water and irrigating land with small expense and great convenience."

During the mid 16th century, rulers in England attempted to attract artisans from other cities (e.g., Venice) by creating England's own patent system. Patents were called *Literae Patere*. This phrase means "open letters," which refers to an open letter of privilege from the government. The English patent system formed the basis of the United States patent system.

Economic Incentive Theory

The original concept of a patent system appears to have been based on the Economic Incentive theory. Economists generally define a public good as both non-rivalrous and non-excludable, which means that consumption of the good by one individual does not reduce the availability of the good for consumption by another individual. Moreover, no individual can be effectively excluded from using the good. The exchange of music and movies files on the Internet is an example of a public good; the use of these files by someone does not restrict the use by anyone else, and there is little effective control over the exchange of these files.

Non-rivalrousness and non-excludability can cause problems for the production of public goods, especially in capital-intensive areas such as the pharmaceutical industry. One could easily imagine the disincentives of researching, developing, and marketing a particular product, if a competitor could simply make and sell the exact product.

The patent system provides a legal mechanism to exclude others from making and selling a patented invention for a limited time and, in theory, provides an incentive to spend resources to research, develop, and market new inventions. The benefits of the patent system include the creation of more inventions, while the costs include the limited diffusion and distribution of such inventions. Ideally, the costs and benefits are carefully balanced by carefully choosing the scope and duration of the intellectual property rights. (For example, patent rights, which have a larger scope, have a much shorter duration than copyrights.)

The Economic Incentive theory also appears to be the basis of IP rights in the U.S. Constitution, which is explored in the next section.

U.S. History

The U.S. Constitution (Art. 1, Sec. 8, Cl. 8) states, "Congress shall have power... to promote the progress of ... useful arts, by securing for limited times to ... Inventors the exclusive rights to their ... Discoveries." The First Congress enacted the Patent Act of 1790, which created the U.S. Patent System and the U.S. Patent Commission. The Secretary of State (Thomas Jefferson), the Secretary of War (Henry Knox), and the Attorney General (Edmund Randolph) were the original three members of the Patent Commission. The first patent was granted on July 30, 1790. This patent was granted to Samuel Hopkins of Philadelphia for a method of producing potash (potassium carbonate), an essential ingredient used in making soap, glass, and gunpowder.

Letter from Thomas Jefferson to Isaac McPherson (August 13, 1813)

If nature has made any one thing less susceptible than all others of exclusive property, it is the action of the thinking power called an idea, which an individual may exclusively possess as long as he keeps it to himself; but the moment it is divulged, it forces itself into the possession of every one, and the receiver cannot dispossess himself of it. Its peculiar character, too, is that no one possesses the less, because every other possesses the whole of it. He who receives an idea from me, receives instruction himself without lessening mine; as he who lights his taper at mine, receives light without darkening me. That ideas should freely spread from one to another over the globe, for the moral and mutual instruction of man, and improvement of his condition, seems to have been peculiarly and benevolently designed by nature, when she made them, like fire, expansible over all space, without lessening their density in any point, and like the air in which we breathe, move, and have our physical being, incapable of confinement or exclusive appropriation. Inventions then cannot, in nature, be a subject of property. Society may [, however,] give an exclusive right to the profits arising from them, as an encouragement to men to pursue ideas which may produce utility....

Contract Theory

In the Contract Theory, the inventors agree to provide full disclosure of their invention to the public (described in a patent application), while the public (through a government agency) agrees to provide exclusive rights to the invention (defined by the claims) to the inventor. The Contract Theory, like the Economic Theory, attempts to solve the public good problem. If inventors did not have the protection of IP rights, they might choose to keep their inventions secret. Publishing patents generally makes the details of new technology publicly available, to be used—or improved upon—by anyone after the patent protection ends.

How Can You Leverage Intellectual Property?

Introduction

The reasons to seek IP rights vary based on the size of the entity (e.g., a "garage" inventor vs. a multi-national corporation), on the industry of the entity (e.g., biotechnology, automotive, publishing), and on the objectives and strategies of the entity. The reasons typically include one or more of the following:

- Protecting a competitive advantage
- Generating licensing revenue from a non-competitor
- Accessing the channels or assets of a competitor
- Deterring a patent infringement lawsuit
- Stimulating an acquisition or an investment
- Providing Leverage in a Negotiation with a Partner
- Preventing others from patenting the technology
- Advertising technical or creative ability and increasing credibility

Protecting a Competitive Advantage

An IP portfolio can create a fence around the core technologies of a company. A core technology might include a feature that moves the price point of the product from a commodity to a premium product, a component that increases performance of the product, a tool or method that reduces manufacturing costs, or a process that enables a unique distribution model. The fence prevents access to the core technologies and forces any competitor to design around the protected technology. In markets that require large capital investments, the mere "patent pending" marking on a product may dissuade a potential competitor from entering the particular market. If the competitor does attempt to enter the particular market, a patent may increase the development time and costs for the competition (due to time and expense spent designing around the protected technology), and may reduce the effectiveness of a competing design. (It will be designed to avoid patent infringement, and not necessarily to provide a particular feature.) Large companies, like Apple, spend lots of time and money protecting their competitive advantage through intellectual property rights (exemplified in the highly publicized Apple vs. Samsung patent infringement lawsuit). Startup companies, however, generally have financial constraints that prevent them from actually enforcing their patent rights.

Generating Licensing Revenue from a Non-Competitor

The technologies of a particular company may be appropriate for products of other companies in different markets or industries. The IP portfolio, under this strategy, can be licensed to other companies to generate revenue without negatively affecting the competitive position of the company. Texas Instruments pioneered this approach some years ago by viewing their patent portfolio as a vehicle for generating significant revenue that would flow to the bottom line of the company. Building on the Texas Instruments model, other companies (e.g., IBM, Rockwell, Dow Chemical, and P&G) have been actively licensing their patents for the purpose of generating additional revenue. Today, revenues from licensing, litigation, and settlements relating to U.S. patents total well over $100 billion. On an annual basis, IBM typically receives more than $1 billion from patent licensing. For startup companies, however, the time and effort to create and execute a licensing program is considered an unwelcomed distraction.

Accessing the Channels or Assets of a Competitor

In some situations, a company might not be able to fully satisfy the demand for their product. According to this strategy, an IP portfolio can be licensed to a competitor to gain access to their manufacturing and distributing channels. Licensing to a competitor would generate an extra profit stream, which just so happens to originate from the bottom line of the competition. This strategy may also be used to increase acceptance and establish (or at least influence) a standard for a technology.

In other situations, a company may need access to the protected technology of a competitor. An IP portfolio can be used as a bargaining tool to gain access to the necessary technology. In this manner, IP acts as a bargaining chip for cross-licensing arrangements or strategic alliances. In 1999, Dell Computer used its patent portfolio to enter a $16 billion cross-licensing deal with IBM. The deal provided Dell with low-cost components, which enabled Dell to avoid millions of dollars in royalty payments to IBM.

Intellectual Property, according to the number one patent holder

Roger Smith, assistant General Counsel for IBM, stated, "You get value from patents in two ways: through fees, and through licensing negotiations that give IBM access to other patents. The

IBM patent portfolio gains us the freedom to do what we need to do through cross-licensing—it gives us access to the inventions of others that are the key to rapid innovation. Access is far more valuable to IBM than the fees it receives from its 9,000 active patents. There's no direct calculation of this value, but it's many times larger than the fee income, perhaps an order of magnitude larger."

Deterring a Patent Infringement Lawsuit

According to the American Intellectual Property Law Association (AIPLA), the average patent infringement lawsuit costs several million dollars. Typically, the cost is similar for both the patent owner *and* the accused infringer. Because of the enormous costs, larger companies often prey on smaller companies by initiating a patent infringement lawsuit that only the larger company can afford. The smaller company can deter such patent infringement by building a patent portfolio that could be infringed by the larger company. Since the larger company has potentially more sales (and hence more liability), they must review the patent portfolio of the smaller company and ensure themselves that the smaller company will not bring a countersuit for patent infringement against them. If the larger company does bring a lawsuit, the smaller company may be able to avoid the high costs of patent litigation by settling out of court with a cross-licensing agreement. A cross-licensing agreement, which could be entered without any exchange of royalty payments, could give the smaller company access to additional technology. Deterring a patent infringement lawsuit is one of the most significant reasons for a startup company to pursue a patent portfolio.

> **Mutually assured destruction**
>
> Large companies with enormous patent portfolios do not typically initiate any offensive action against each other because of the potential retaliation. This "mutually assured destruction" situation occurs in the automotive and computer industries; the companies in these industries simply stockpile patents. Patent portfolios, in these situations, are valued more on their quantity than their quality.

Stimulating an Acquisition or Investment

Larger companies (e.g., Google) often acquire smaller companies based solely on their ownership of an essential piece of IP. Larger companies can duplicate the effort, intelligence, and drive of a startup company; however, they cannot make, use, or sell the patented invention of a startup without acquiring the rights from the startup. In many situations, acquiring the rights means acquiring the entire company. For similar reasons, IP may also stimulate a funding event by an angel investor or a venture capitalist. The investor may view the IP as an asset that could stimulate an acquisition in the future or, at the very least, can be sold if the startup fails (thereby mitigating some of the risk of the investment). Stimulating an acquisition or increasing valuation during an investment is one of the other most significant reasons for a startup company to pursue a patent portfolio.

Providing Leverage in a Negotiation with a Partner

Often, when startup companies and large companies enter a partnership (known as a Joint Development Agreement or

"JDA"), the agreement of their partnership will identify "background" technologies that are owned by the two companies before the commencement of the JDA and excluded from the shared provisions of the JDA. By filing patent applications on the relevant background technologies before the commencement of the JDA, startups can benefit from greater leverage in a negotiation with a partner after the conclusion of the JDA.

Preventing Others from Patenting the Technology

Although not typically a stand-alone reason, the patenting of a particular technology does prevent others from patenting the technology. There are more inexpensive ways to accomplish this same goal (e.g., publishing an article on the invention), but large companies often cite this strategy as a supplement to other strategies.

Advertising Technical and Creative Ability and Increasing Credibility

A "patent pending" or "patented" marking indicates to consumers (sometimes incorrectly) that the product is unique and cannot be obtained anywhere else. At the very least, a patent can signal the innovation and enhance the technological prestige of a company.

Chapter Two

How Does the Patent System Work?

Korekiyo Takahashi, who would later become the twentieth Prime Minister of Japan, was sent to the United States in the late nineteenth century. He later stated, "We have looked to see what nations are the greatest, so that we can be like them. We asked ourselves what is it that makes the United States such a great nation? We investigated and we found that it [is] patents, and we will have patents" (K. Takahashi, First Director General of JPO, appointed 1885)

Chapter Contents

- Types of Patent Protection
    - Introduction
    - Utility Patents
    - Design Patents
    - Plant Patents
- Steps of the Patent Process
    - Introduction
    - Filing a Patent Application and Formal Examination
    - Publication
    - Search and Substantive Examination
    - Grant
- Sections of a Utility Patent
    - Introduction
    - Front Page
    - Specification
    - Claims

Types of Patent Protection

Introduction

There are three types of patents: utility, design, and plant. The United States Patent and Trademark Office (USPTO or PTO) has granted over 8,000,000 utility patents, over 600,000 design patents, and over 20,000 plant patents. The utility patent, being the most common, is the "default" patent type. When someone refers to a "patent," he or she is most likely referring to a "utility patent." After this chapter, "patent" will be used to refer to a "utility patent."

Utility Patents

The utility patent covers any "process, machine, manufacture, or composition of matter." Here are a couple of examples:

- Process—U.S. Pat. No. 135,245 issued to Pasteur in 1873 for a process for brewing beer and U.S. Pat. No. 6,878,885 assigned to Weight Watchers in 2005 for a process for controlling body weight
- Machine—U.S. Pat. No. 821,393 issued to Orville and Wilbur Wright in 1906 for a machine that flies and U.S. Pat. No. 6,651,766 issued to Dean Kamen in 2003 for a personal mobility vehicle (sold under the "Segway" trademark)
- Manufacture—U.S. Pat. No. 2,717,437 issued to Mestral in 1955 for a velvet type fabric (sold under the "Velcro" trademark) and U.S. Pat. No. 4,289,794 assigned to General Mills in 1981 for a gasified candy (sold under the "Pop Rocks" trademark)

- Composition of Matter—U.S. Pat. No. 644,077 issued to Hoffmann in 1900 for acetylsalicylic acid (sold under the "Aspirin" trademark) and U.S. Pat. No. 4,736,866 assigned to Harvard on 1988 for a transgenic non-human mammal (and known as the Harvard Mouse).

In the early years of the United States Patent and Trademark Office (USPTO), patents were granted at a rate of about 20 per year. In 2005, patents were granted at a rate of more than 3,000 per week; as shown in the chart of Figure 1, patents are granted at an increasing rate.

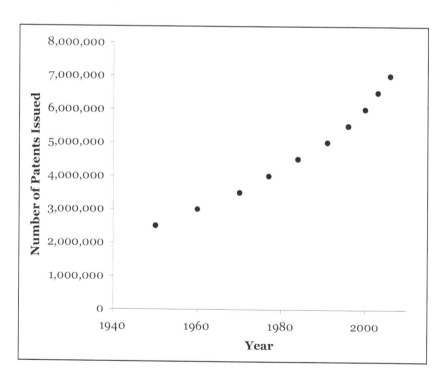

Figure 1. Approximate year for various issued patents

The coverage that the utility patent provides is determined by the claims. Therefore, the test for infringement of a utility patent includes interpreting the claims and comparing the interpreted claims with the accused product or method.

Comment on the scope of the "light bulb patent" and the "one-click patent"

The media, and hence the public, are both often confused by the scope of the coverage of a patent. It is not uncommon to read about Edison's "light bulb patent" or Amazon's "one-click patent." It is a common misconception that the former might cover *every* light bulb, or that the latter might cover *every time users click with their mouse just once*. In fact, as stated above, the protection that the utility patent provides is determined by the claims. According to the claims, Edison's "light bulb patent" covers only "an electric lamp ... consisting of a filament of carbon of high resistance ... secured to metallic wires." The Amazon patent covers only "a method of placing an order for an item comprising ... displaying information identifying the item; and in response to only a single action being performed, sending a request to order the item along with an identifier of a purchaser of the item to a server system ... retrieving additional information previously stored for the purchaser...; and generating an order to purchase the requested item for the purchaser ... using the retrieved additional information; and fulfilling the generated order to complete purchase of the item, whereby the item is ordered without using a shopping cart ordering model."

Design Patents

A design patent, also known as "industrial designs" outside the United States, covers the ornamental or aesthetic features of a product. Here are a few examples:

- U.S. Des. No. 150,683 issued to Charles Eames in 1948 for the "LCW" chair
- U.S. Des. No. 86,754 issued to Strauss in 1932 for the "Golden Gate" bridge
- U.S. Des. No. 199,433 issued to Ferdinand Porsche in 1964 for the "Porsche 911"
- U.S. Des. No. 499,112 assigned to Apple Computer in 2004 for their "OSX Hard drive icon"

The test for infringement of a design patent includes the "ordinary observer" test, which states that "[I]f, in the eye of an ordinary observer, giving such attention as a purchaser usually gives, two designs are substantially the same, if the resemblance is such as to deceive such an observer, inducing him to purchase one supposing it to be the other, the first one patented is infringed by the other" *Gorham Co. v. White*, 81 U.S. 511 (1871).

Unlike utility patents, design patents do not cover the functionality of a product—only the ornamental or aesthetic features. Consider two products that have the exact same functions. If the second product is designed to look completely different, it does not infringe on the design patent of the first product. In contrast to a utility patent (which usually takes 2–5 years and costs ~$40,000), a design patent is relatively fast (1–2 years) and cheap (~$2,000) to obtain.

Trademark law offers protection on the look and feel of the packaging (called "trade dress") of a product if it acquires a "secondary meaning" or "acquires distinctiveness," which is typically gained over an extended time period through advertising or massive exposure. Two great examples of trade dress include the triangular shape of the packaging for Toblerone chocolates and the contoured shape of the bottle for Coca-Cola soda. In contrast to trade dress, which can potentially last forever, design patents do not require secondary meaning or acquired distinctiveness; instead, design patents expire after 14 years and enter the public domain.

In contrast with copyright (protection of the artistic expression), design patents offer a broader scope (protection on multiple embodiments or variations), but a limited term (14 years for a design patent compared with life of the author plus 70 years). In further contrast, copyright protection does not require novelty or non-obviousness over prior artistic expression. However, copyright protection does not offer protection against later artistic expressions that were independently created.

Plant Patents

A plant patent covers asexually reproduced plants, such as cultivated sports, mutants, hybrids, and newly found seedlings. Asexually propagated plants are reproduced without seeds, such as by the rooting of cuttings, by layering, budding, grafting, or inarching. Plant patents do not cover tuber-propagated plant (e.g., the Irish potato and the Jerusalem artichoke) or a plant found in an uncultivated state. Like a utility patent, the plant patent lasts for a term of 20 years from the filing date (or the earliest priority date).

Steps of the Patent Process

Introduction

The USPTO, which is an agency of the U.S. Department of Commerce, administers the patent and trademark laws. It examines patent and trademark applications, grants patents and registers trademarks, and maintains a search facility and database of patents and trademarks. In some respects, the USPTO is the scientific and technical counterpart to the Library of Congress. Through the preservation, classification, and dissemination of patent information, the USPTO aids and encourages scientific and technical advancement.

The USPTO has no jurisdiction, however, over questions of the infringement and enforcement of patents or trademarks. Parties cannot complain to the USPTO about infringement issues— parties can only bring an infringement lawsuit (typically in federal court).

USPTO by the numbers

The United States Patent and Trademark Office has over 6,000 employees; about half of these employees are either examiners or other workers with technical and legal training. Patent applications are filed at a rate of more than 1,000 applications per day, and patents are issued at a rate of more than 3,000 every week (always on a Tuesday).

As shown in Figure 2, there are generally four steps in the patent process: (A) Filing of a Patent Application and Formal Examination; (B) Publication; (C) Search and Substantive Examination; and (D) Grant.

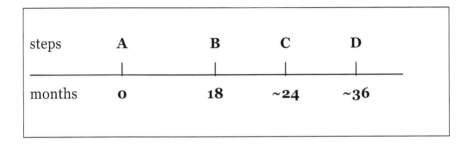

Figure 2. Steps in the patent process

Filing a Patent Application and Formal Examination

A complete patent application (which is clumsily referred to as a "non-provisional" patent application) includes:

- A specification that includes a written description of the invention and drawings (if necessary for the understanding of the invention),
- At least one claim to define the scope of protection and coverage of the patent,
- A declaration by the inventors that—to the best of their knowledge—they are the first inventor of the subject matter of the patent application, and
- Government fees, including filing, search, and examination fees.

After the patent application is filed, the patent office examines the application to ensure that it complies with the administrative requirements and formalities (e.g., that all relevant documentation is included and the application fee has been paid). The patent application is not assigned an official filing date until the specification (with any necessary drawings) and at least one claim are filed with the USPTO. The declaration and the government fee may be filed later (without affecting the filing date), if accompanied with the required late fee.

Comment on models, exhibits, and specimens

During the early years of the patent system, the USPTO required models or exhibits of the subject matter of the patent applications. Now, the USPTO may require a working model or other physical exhibit only if deemed necessary. This is very rare. A patent application for an alleged perpetual motion device, however, is another matter. The USPTO typically requires a working model in the case of perpetual motion devices.

Publication

Unless specifically instructed otherwise, the USPTO publishes patent applications 18 months after the earliest priority date. The publication of patent applications is not a grant of any patent rights. An applicant does not have any rights over his or her invention until after the pending application has been allowed and granted (or "issued"); it is simply a publication of the patent application (e.g., an article in a technical journal). Although a patent owner cannot sue an infringer until a patent has been issued, recovery of post-publication and pre-issuance damages is possible if two conditions are met. First, the alleged infringer must have had actual notice of the published application. Second, the claims of the published patent application must be substantially identical to the infringed claims in the issued patent. For this reason, once the patent application is published, the applicant may benefit from informing potential infringers of their pending patent application.

The publication of patent applications allows for a better understanding of the technical advancements of a competitor. But, more importantly, the publication of patent applications also allows for more effective searches of the current state of the art. Not long ago, before the publication of patent applications, pending applications were kept secret (even to other Examiners at the USPTO) until they were granted. Since patent applications can be pending for several years, not publishing the patent applications prevented the Examiners from finding relevant prior art, so the Examiners issued patent applications on otherwise unpatentable inventions.

Comment

In the United States, the publication of a *pending application* is confusingly similar to the publication of an *issued patent*. Pending applications typically have an 11-digit number that starts with the publication year (e.g., 2003/0095096 for patent application on the Apple iPod click wheel), while issued patents typically have 7-digit (or fewer) number (e.g., U.S. Patent

---

Number 7,345,671 for the issued patent on the Apple iPod click wheel). The published applications and issued patents look very similar, but they are dramatically different—one is simply a publication of the pending application, while the other is a grant of patent rights in an issued patent. For this reason, be extra careful when first reviewing a patent document.

Search and Substantive Examination

After the patent application passes through the convoluted process at the USPTO and rises to the top of a queue, the patent office conducts a search to determine the prior art in the specific field to which the invention relates. Prior art is all information (e.g., issued patents, published applications, technical publications, and sold products) in both the United States and in other countries that has been disclosed to the public in any form before a given date. The results of the search are used during the substantive examination to compare the invention of the patent application with the prior art.

The aim of the substantive examination is to ensure that the application satisfies the patentability requirements. In order for an invention to be considered patentable, the patent application must cover proper subject matter (known as the "proper subject matter" requirement) and must teach someone skilled in the art to make and use the invention (known as the "enablement requirement). Both of these requirements are explored in Chapter Three. The invention of the patent application must also be useful, new, and not an obvious combination or modification of the prior art (known as the "utility," "novelty," and "unobviousness" requirements), which are explored in Chapter Four. Finally, the patent application must be filed within certain time limits (known as the "statutory bars" or, within this book, as the "timing requirements"), which are explored in Chapter Five.

Once the application has been examined, the results of the examination are sent to the applicant in a document called an "office action"— an *action* taken by the Patent *Office*. An office action typically includes several rejections, including:

- The invention, as defined in the claims, has been described in the prior art (and therefore fails the novelty requirement),
- The invention, as defined in the claims, is an obvious combination or modification of the prior art (and therefore fails the non-obviousness requirement), and
- The invention, as defined in the claims, is not described in a manner that allows someone to make and use the invention (and therefore fails the enablement requirement).

In response to the office action, an applicant may modify (or "amend") the claims of the patent application, present an argument against the rejections, or both amend the claims and argue the rejections. The document with these amendments and/or arguments is typically called an "office action response" (or simply "response"). The back-and-forth process in which the USPTO sends an office action that rejects the claims and the applicant sends a response that amends or argues the claims (i.e., "prosecution") typically repeats two or three times before the patent application is allowed or finally rejected. In fact, because the prosecution process is considered a negotiation with the USPTO, patent applications that have been accepted without any rejections are often suspected of having too narrow of patent scope.

Comment on the amendments to the patent application

The applicant may change the scope of the claims of the patent application as long as the originally filed specification supports the changes. The specification (i.e., the written description and the drawings) can be changed only to correct inaccuracies of description and definition or unnecessary words, and to provide substantial correspondence between the claims, the description, and the drawing. The changes cannot include new matter beyond the originally filed specification. Matter not found in the originally filed specification cannot be added to the application and can be claimed only in a separate application.

Grant

If the Examiners determine all requirements have been met, the patent office allows the patent application and grants (or "issues") a patent. For several decades, the typical allowance rate (i.e., the ratio of the number of patent applications granted to the number of patent applications filed) was about 60% to 70%. As noted in Figure 3, the allowance rate has dropped significantly in the early 2000s. In August 2012, according to the USPTO, the allowance rate was approximately 50%.

Figure 3. Allowance Rates for fiscal years 1975–2008

Many patent offices outside of the United States provide a period during which third parties may oppose the grant of a patent based on prior art. Opposition proceedings may be pre-grant and/or post-grant, and are allowed within the specified time limits. As of the writing of this version of this text, Congress has enacted statutes that would implement a similar opposition procedure.

Once a patent has been issued, there are methods of correcting or amending the patent. These methods include a certificate of correction, a reissue application, and a reexamination of the patent. The certificate of correction is generally used for smaller typographical errors, while a reissue application is generally used for defects that make the patent inoperative or invalid (e.g., the claims being too broad or too narrow). A reexamination is generally used when newly discovered prior art raises an issue of potential unpatentability, and can be filed by the patent owner or another entity (e.g., a competitor or a disgruntled employee).

Comment on patent law's biggest misconception

The grant of a patent provides the applicant with the right to exclude others from making, using, or selling the patented invention. A patent grant does *not* provide any rights to the applicants to make, use, or sell the invention themselves. Many inventors do not understand this difference, which can lead to disastrous results. This misconception is explored in subsequent chapters.

Sections of a Patent

Introduction

The actual documents for published applications and issued patents have three major functions: (1) to provide details about the inventor and the owner; (2) to describe the nature of the invention, including how to make and use the invention; and (3) to define the legal scope of the patent documents. These three major functions are accomplished in three corresponding sections: front page, specification, and claims.

Front Page

The front page of both published applications and issued patents includes the Title, the name of the Inventor and the Assignee, and an Abstract. The Title and Abstract merely aid in the classification and search of the patent documents; they have no legal significance. The Inventor and Assignee state the inventor and the owner, respectively, at the time of either the *publication* of the application or the *issuance* of the patent. This information, on the front page, is never updated (and is often out of date months after the publication or issuance date). The current information on the owner of the patent is in the Assignment Records of the patent office.

Specification

The specification, which is often considered the "technical section" of the patent, includes the drawings and the detailed description. The specification of a patent application must meet the enablement requirement by describing the invention in sufficient detail so that anyone skilled in the same technical field could make and use the invention without further inventive effort or excessive experimentation. If this requirement is not met, the patent may not be granted or may be revoked after it is challenged in a court action.

Claims

The claims, which make up the "legal section" of the patent, define the scope of protection and coverage of a patent. The claims are absolutely crucial to a patented invention. Poorly drafted claims may lead to a worthless patent, even for a truly valuable invention, which is easy to circumvent or design around. The claims are the basis on whether the invention satisfies the novelty and non-obviousness requirements. The claims are also the basis on whether another product or method infringes that patent. In patent litigation, interpreting the claims is generally the first step in determining whether the patent is valid and whether the patent has been infringed.

Chapter Three

What Is the Invention?

Chapter Contents

- Subject Matter Requirement
  - Introduction
  - Statute
  - Case Law
- Written Description Requirement
  - Statute
  - Case Law on the Enablement Rule
  - Case Law on the Best Mode Rule

Subject Matter Requirement

Introduction

In order for an invention to be considered patentable, it must meet several requirements for both the characteristics of the invention and the preparation of the patent application. Regarding the characteristics of the invention, the invention must meet the *proper subject matter* requirement and must satisfy the three fundamental patentability requirements: *usefulness, novelty*, and *non-obviousness*. In this chapter, the discussion explores the proper subject matter requirement; Chapter Four addresses the three fundamental patentability requirements. Regarding the preparation of the patent application, the patent application must meet the written description requirement, the enablement requirement, and the best mode requirement (explored in this chapter) and must be filed on a timely basis (explored in Chapter Five).

Statute

According to the Patent Laws, the proper subject matter of patentable inventions is defined as "any ... process, machine, manufacture, ... composition of matter, or ... improvement thereof" (35 U.S.C. 101). For an invention to meet the proper subject matter requirement, it must fall within one of these four statutory categories.

The machine, manufacture, and composition of matter categories all generally include tangible inventions (or "things") and, for this reason, are generally considered a single category. The process category, on the other hand, includes intangible inventions (e.g., a series of steps or actions) and is differentiated in the patent laws from the other categories. A process may include a method of manufacturing, a method of processing information (known as "software patents"), or a method of distributing or selling something (known as "business method patents"). These last two examples of the process category have generated enormous controversy. In some situations, an invention may be patented as a product and a method of either manufacturing or using the product. In fact, a simple search through the records of the USPTO reveals hundreds of thousands of issued patents with both the words "Method" and "System" in the title of the issued patent.

Case Law

The following section includes several court decisions on what may be considered proper subject matter. This section includes an excerpt from the 1980 Supreme Court case of *Diamond v. Chakrabarty*. This case is an important example of case law because it relates to the proper subject matter requirement; specifically, this case examines the question of whether or not human-made micro-organisms qualify as patentable subject matter.

Diamond v. Chakrabarty (Supreme Court 1980)

Mr. Chief Justice Burger for the Supreme Court of the United States:

I

In 1972, respondent Chakrabarty, a microbiologist, filed a patent application, assigned to the General Electric Co. The application asserted 36 claims related to Chakrabarty's invention of "a bacterium from the genus Pseudomonas containing therein at least two stable energy-generating plasmids, each of said plasmids providing a separate hydrocarbon degradative pathway." This human-made, genetically engineered bacterium is capable of breaking down multiple components of crude oil. Because of this property, which is possessed by no naturally occurring bacteria, Chakrabarty's invention is believed to have significant value for the treatment of oil spills.

Chakrabarty's patent claims were of three types: first, process claims for the method of producing the bacteria; second, claims for an inoculum comprised of a carrier material floating on water, such as straw, and the new bacteria; and third, claims to the bacteria themselves. The patent examiner allowed the claims falling into the first two categories, but rejected claims for the bacteria. His decision rested on two grounds: (1) that micro-organisms are "products of nature," and (2) that as living things they are not patentable subject matter under 35 U.S.C. 101.

...

II

The Constitution grants Congress broad power to legislate to "promote the Progress of Science and useful Arts, by securing for limited Times to Authors and Inventors the exclusive Right to their respective Writings and Discoveries." The patent laws promote this progress by offering inventors exclusive rights for a limited period as an incentive for their inventiveness and research efforts. The authority of Congress is exercised in the hope that "[t]he productive effort thereby fostered will have a positive effect on society through the introduction of new products and processes of manufacture into the economy, and the emanations by way of increased employment and better lives for our citizens."

The question before us in this case is a narrow one of statutory interpretation requiring us to construe 35 U.S.C. 101, which provides:

> "Whoever invents or discovers any new and useful process, machine, manufacture, or composition of matter, or any new and useful improvement thereof, may obtain a patent therefor, subject to the conditions and requirements of this title."

Specifically, we must determine whether respondent's microorganism constitutes a "manufacture" or "composition of matter" within the meaning of the statute.

III

...

This Court has read the term "manufacture" in 101 in accordance with its dictionary definition to mean "the production of articles for use from raw or prepared materials by giving to these materials new forms, qualities, properties, or combinations, whether by hand-labor or by machinery." Similarly, "composition of matter" has been construed consistent with its common usage to include "all compositions of two or more substances and . . . all composite articles, whether they be the results of chemical union, or of mechanical mixture, or whether they be gases, fluids, powders or solids." In choosing such expansive terms as "manufacture" and "composition of matter," modified by the comprehensive "any," Congress plainly contemplated that the patent laws would be given wide scope.

The relevant legislative history also supports a broad construction. The Patent Act of 1793, authored by Thomas Jefferson, defined statutory subject matter as "any new and useful art, machine, manufacture, or composition of matter, or any new or useful improvement [thereof]." The Act embodied Jefferson's philosophy that "ingenuity should receive a liberal encouragement." Subsequent patent statutes in 1836, 1870, and 1874 employed this same broad language. In 1952, when the patent laws were recodified, Congress replaced the word "art" with "process," but otherwise left Jefferson's language intact. The Committee Reports accompanying the 1952 Act inform us that

Congress intended statutory subject matter to "include anything under the sun that is made by man."

This is not to suggest that 101 has no limits or that it embraces every discovery. The laws of nature, physical phenomena, and abstract ideas have been held not patentable. See *Funk Brothers Seed Co. v. Kalo Inoculant Co.*, 333 U.S. 127, 130 (1948). Thus, a new mineral discovered in the earth or a new plant found in the wild is not patentable subject matter. Likewise, Einstein could not patent his celebrated law that $E=mc^2$.; nor could Newton have patented the law of gravity. Such discoveries are "manifestations of . . . nature, free to all men and reserved exclusively to none."

Judged in this light, respondent's micro-organism plainly qualifies as patentable subject matter. His claim is not to a hitherto unknown natural phenomenon, but to a nonnaturally occurring manufacture or composition of matter—a product of human ingenuity "having a distinctive name, character [and] use." The point is underscored dramatically by comparison of the invention here with that in the *Funk* case. There, the patentee had discovered that there existed in nature certain species of root-nodule bacteria which did not exert a mutually inhibitive effect on each other. He used that discovery to produce a mixed culture capable of inoculating the seeds of leguminous plants. Concluding that the patentee had discovered "only some of the handiwork of nature," the Court ruled the product nonpatentable:

"Each of the species of root-nodule bacteria contained in the package infects the same group of leguminous plants which it always infected. No species acquires a different use. The combination of species produces no new bacteria, no change in the six species of bacteria, and no enlargement of the range of their utility. Each species has the same effect it always had. The bacteria perform in their natural way. Their use in combination does not improve in any way their natural functioning. They serve the ends nature originally provided and act quite independently of any effort of the patentee."

Here, by contrast, the patentee has produced a new bacterium with markedly different characteristics from any found in nature and one having the potential for significant utility. His discovery is not nature's handiwork, but his own; accordingly it is patentable subject matter under 101.

...

IV (B)

The petitioner's second argument is that micro-organisms cannot qualify as patentable subject matter until Congress expressly authorizes such protection. His position rests on the fact that genetic technology was unforeseen when Congress enacted 101. From this it is argued that resolution of the patentability of inventions such as respondent's should be left to Congress. The legislative process, the petitioner argues, is best equipped to weigh the competing economic, social, and scientific considerations involved, and to determine whether living organisms produced by genetic engineering should receive patent protection. In support of this position, the petitioner relies on our recent holding in *Parker v. Flook*, 437 U.S. 584 (1978), and the statement that the judiciary "must proceed cautiously when . . . asked to extend patent rights into areas wholly unforeseen by Congress."

It is, of course, correct that Congress, not the courts, must define the limits of patentability; but it is equally true that once Congress has spoken it is "the province and duty of the judicial department to say what the law is." Congress has performed its constitutional role in defining patentable subject matter in 101; we perform ours in construing the language Congress has employed. In so doing, our obligation is to take statutes as we find them, guided, if ambiguity appears, by the legislative history and statutory purpose. Here, we perceive no ambiguity. The subject-matter provisions of the patent law have been cast in broad terms to fulfill the constitutional and statutory goal of promoting "the Progress of Science and the useful Arts" with all that means for the social and economic benefits envisioned by Jefferson. Broad general language is not necessarily ambiguous when congressional objectives require broad terms.

...

A rule that unanticipated inventions are without protection would conflict with the core concept of the patent law that anticipation undermines patentability. The inventions most benefiting mankind are those that "push back the frontiers of chemistry, physics, and the like." Congress employed broad general language in drafting 101 precisely because such inventions are often unforeseeable.

To buttress his argument, the petitioner, with the support of amicus, points to grave risks that may be generated by research endeavors such as respondent's. The briefs present a gruesome parade of horribles. Scientists, among them Nobel laureates, are quoted suggesting that genetic research may pose a serious threat to the human race, or, at the very least, that the dangers are far too substantial to permit such research to proceed apace at this time. We are told that genetic research and related technological developments may spread pollution and disease, that it may result in a loss of genetic diversity, and that its practice may tend to depreciate the value of human life. These arguments are forcefully, even passionately, presented; they remind us that, at times, human ingenuity seems unable to control fully the forces it creates—that, with Hamlet, it is sometimes better "to bear those ills we have than fly to others that we know not of."

It is argued that this Court should weigh these potential hazards in considering whether respondent's invention is patentable subject matter under 101. We disagree. The grant or denial of patents on micro-organisms is not likely to put an end to genetic research or to its attendant risks. The large amount of research that has already occurred when no researcher had sure knowledge that patent protection would be available suggests that legislative or judicial fiat as to patentability will not deter the scientific mind from probing into the unknown any more than

Canute could command the tides. Whether respondent's claims are patentable may determine whether research efforts are accelerated by the hope of reward or slowed by want of incentives, but that is all.

What is more important is that we are without competence to entertain these arguments—either to brush them aside as fantasies generated by fear of the unknown, or to act on them. The choice we are urged to make is a matter of high policy for resolution within the legislative process after the kind of investigation, examination, and study that legislative bodies can provide and courts cannot. That process involves the balancing of competing values and interests, which in our democratic system is the business of elected representatives. Whatever their validity, the contentions now pressed on us should be addressed to the political branches of the Government, the Congress and the Executive, and not to the courts.

We have emphasized in the recent past that "[o]ur individual appraisal of the wisdom or unwisdom of a particular [legislative] course ... is to be put aside in the process of interpreting a statute." Our task, rather, is the narrow one of determining what Congress meant by the words it used in the statute; once that is done our powers are exhausted. Congress is free to amend 101 so as to exclude from patent protection organisms produced by genetic engineering. Compare, for example, 42 U.S.C. 2181 (a), which exempt from patent protection inventions "useful solely in the utilization of special nuclear material or atomic energy in an atomic weapon." Or it may choose to craft a statute specifically designed for such living things. But, until Congress takes such action, this Court must construe the language of 101 as it is. The language of that section fairly embraces respondent's invention.

Accordingly, the judgment of the Court of Customs and Patent Appeals is Affirmed.

In *Parke-Davis & Co. v. H.K. Mulford Co.* (C.C.S.D.N.Y. 1911), Parke-Davis owned two patents on a process for extracting and isolating purified Adrenalin from the suprarenal glands of an animal. Mulford asserted that the patents were invalid as improper subject matter. The court held that a *process* of isolating a natural substance can qualify as proper subject matter under 35 U.S.C. 101 and stated that "It became for every practical purpose a new thing commercially and therapeutically."

In *General Electric Co. v. DeForest Radio Co.* (3d Cir. 1928), the court held that a claim on "substantially pure tungsten" is invalid as not proper subject matter. The court stated that "What [the patentee] produced by his process was natural tungsten in substantially pure form. What he discovered were natural qualities of pure tungsten. Manifestly he did not create pure tungsten, nor did he create its characteristics. These were created by nature...."

In *State Street Bank & Trust Co. v. Signature Financial Group, Inc.* (Fed. Cir. 1998), the Court of Appeals for the Federal Circuit held that a data processing system for managing a hub-and-spoke mutual fund configuration can qualify as proper subject matter. The court stated that "the mere fact that a claimed invention involves inputting numbers, calculating numbers, outputting numbers, and storing numbers... would not render it [improper] subject matter, unless... its operation does not produce a useful, concrete and tangible result." The *State Street Bank* case created an explosion of patent applications on business method inventions in the late 1990s during the first Internet boom. Most of these business method inventions are related to e-commerce.

In re Bilski (Supreme Court 2010)

In early summer 2010, the Supreme Court issued their opinion on the "Bilski" case for business method and software patents. While the Court denied patent protection for the Bilski invention (which covered a procedure for instructing buyers and sellers how to protect against the risk of price fluctuations), the Court ruled that both business methods and software can be eligible subject matter under the law. The Court supported the machine-or-transformation test for an invention that includes a method or process, but stated that it is not the only test.

To satisfy the machine prong of the machine-or-transformation test, the process must be tied to a particular machine. The machine must implement the process, and cannot merely be an object upon which the process operates. (e.g. "A method of installing a refrigerator" does not satisfy the machine prong even though a refrigerator is undeniably a machine.) Finally, the machine must provide "meaningful limits on the scope of the claims."

To satisfy the transformation prong of the test, the process has to transform a particular article. "Transform" means to change to a different state or thing. An article, as defined under the machine-or-transformation test, is either a physical object or substance, or electronic data that represents a physical object or substance. For example, the definition of "article" includes signals representing a patient's heart activity, signals representing seismic activity, or data representing images. Organizational relationships, legal rights and obligations, and business risks are not articles. A court held, for instance, that a credit card is not an article as required by the machine-or-transformation test because the card is an abstraction of "a credit card account, which is a series of rights and obligations existing between an account holder or account holders and a card issuer." Finally, forecasts and notifications are not articles as defined by the machine-or-transformation test.

What is a Software Patent?

The question seems simple enough, but the answer is quite complex. There is no "check box" for patent applications on software inventions. In fact, the patent laws do not even mention the word "software". Patent applications are roughly divided into (1) devices and systems that include separate components and (2) processes and methods that include separate steps. Software is generally thought of as separate steps that form a process. One example is the steps that form the RSA encryption (one of the most prevalent encryption techniques, developed at MIT). The confusing part is that these methods can often be re-abstracted as a system. In fact, most of the claims of the RSA encryption patent are not for "methods", but rather for "systems" that include means for encoding or registering.

So, where do patents on software end and other patents on manufacturing methods or even systems begin? Like most aspects of the law, this area involves shades of grey that engineers often cannot see. Lawyers are skilled at working in this grey area. In the patent of the *Diamond v. Chakrabarty* Supreme Court case, the patent attorney was able to envision the Chakrabarty invention as both (1) a bacteria, and (2) a process for producing bacteria. Given this, can an invention ever be labeled as a "software patent"?

Written Description Requirement

Statute

According to the Patent Laws, the specification shall contain a *written description* of the invention, and of the manner and process of making and using it, in such full, clear, concise, and exact terms as to *enable* any person skilled in the art to which it pertains... to make and use the [invention], and shall set forth the *best mode* contemplated by the inventor of carrying out his invention. (35 U.S.C. 112, 1st paragraph).

Case Law on the Enablement Rule

The specification of an invention must meet the *enablement requirement* by describing the invention in sufficient detail so that anyone skilled in the same technical field could reconstruct and practice the invention without further inventive effort or excessive experimentation. By requiring the enablement of any person skilled in the art to make and use the subject matter of every claim, this enablement rule of section 112 prevents *overly broad* claims that stretch beyond what the inventor could imagine. This rule does not require that everyone be enabled by the specification—only those skilled in the art.

In the 1890s, the USPTO issued U.S. Pat. No. 317,076 to Sawyer and Man for an electric light. The patent included a claim for "An incandescent conductor for an electric lamp, of carbonized fibrous or textile material...." The specification enabled only the making and using of carbonized paper and wood, which was never a commercial success. Thomas Edison, after rejecting over 30 carbonized woods as unsuitable, sold an electric lamp with carbonized bamboo and the Electro-Dynamic Light Company (owners of the '076 patent) sued the Edison Electric Light Company. In *The Incandescent Lamp Patent* case (1895), the Supreme Court ruled that the broad claims of the '076 patent, directed to carbonized fibrous or textile material, were invalid under section 112 as not being enabled by the written description. The Court stated that "If the description be so vague and uncertain that no one can tell, except by independent experiments, how to construct the patented device, the patent is void."

According to *In re Wands* (Fed. Cir. 1988), "Enablement is not precluded by the necessity for some experimentation such as routine screening. However, experimentation needed to practice the invention must not be *undue experimentation*" (emphasis added). The court further stated the factors to be considered in determining whether a disclosure would require undue experimentation:

- Quantity of experimentation necessary,
- Amount of direction or guidance presented,
- Presence or absence of working examples,
- Nature of the invention,
- State of the prior art,
- Relative skill of those in the art,
- Predictability or unpredictability of the art, and
- Breadth of the claims.

Case Law on the Best Mode Rule

The specification must meet the *best mode* requirement by describing the mode or embodiment of the invention that the inventor considered to be the best *at the time of filing the application*. A typical patent application will include several variations (called "embodiments"). The best mode requirement does not require the applicant to indicate which of the embodiments is the best, and does not require the inventor to update or revise the patent application or issued patent if improvements are made to the invention after the filing of the patent application. The best mode rule of section 112 prevents the patentee from withholding information (e.g., a trade secret) from the public.

As declared by the Federal Circuit in *Bayer AG v. Schein Pharmaceuticals Inc.* (Fed. Cir. 2002), best mode violations are found where there is either a "failure to disclose a preferred embodiment, or ... failure to disclose a preference that materially affected making or using the invention." The two-part test, as set forth by the court, states as follows:

(1) The factfinder must determine whether, at the time the patent application was filed, the inventor had a best mode of practicing the claimed invention—whether there was a preferred way to build or use the claimed device or process. This inquiry is entirely subjective.

(2) If there is a best mode, a court will inquire whether "the disclosure [in the patent specification] is adequate to enable one of ordinary skill in the art to practice the best mode of the invention. This inquiry is objective and depends upon the scope of the claimed invention and the level of skill in the relevant art" (insert page number for direct quotation here).

Note that not every preference constitutes a best mode—only the "preferences that are reflected in a preferred embodiment or that relate to making or using the invention and have a material effect on the properties of the claimed invention must be disclosed." For example, a typical patent application for a mechanical device does not need to include CAD drawings, and a typical patent application for a software algorithm does not need to include actual code.

Comment on Best Mode Requirement

The inventor is not required to indicate which of the described embodiments is the best or update the specification if the best mode changes. Therefore, the satisfaction of the best mode requirement is very difficult to ascertain. Costly and time-consuming litigation is typically the only way to enforce this requirement. Nevertheless, there is good reason for this requirement to exist. The monopoly granted by a patent is in exchange for the complete disclosure of the invention to the public. If an applicant has not disclosed the best mode of the invention, and has instead intended to hold the best mode as a (trade) secret, they should not receive a monopoly in exchange.

Chapter Four

Is the Invention Patentable?

"What is *novel, nonobvious* or *useful* is hard enough to know in a relatively stable field. In a transforming market [such as the Internet], it's nearly impossible for anyone—let alone an underpaid worker in the U.S. Department of Commerce who spends on average of eight hours evaluating the prior art in a patent and gets paid based on how many he processes—to identify what's *novel*."—Lawrence Lessig

Chapter Contents

- Introduction
- Utility Requirement
  - Introduction and Statute
  - Case Law
- Novelty Requirement
  - Introduction and Statute
  - Tips for Understanding the Novelty Requirement
  - Case Law
- Non-Obviousness Requirement
  - Introduction and Statute
  - Tips for Understanding the Non-Obviousness Requirement
  - Case Law
  - Teaching, Suggestion, or Motivation
  - Secondary Considerations
- How to Conduct a Patentability Search
  - Introduction
  - Primary Search Tools
  - Secondary Search Tools
  - Recommended Search Strategy

Introduction

For an invention to be deemed patentable, the claims of the patent application on the invention must meet the three main patentability requirements: utility, novelty, and non-obviousness. This chapter discusses these three requirements, and it concludes with a guide to conducting a patentability investigation.

Utility Requirement

Introduction and Statute

According to the patent statutes, "Whoever invents or discovers any new and useful [invention] may obtain a patent thereon, subject to the conditions and requirements of this title" (35 U.S.C. 101). It is debated whether the drafters of this statute meant for "new and useful" to be a requirement, especially considering the "subject to the condition and requirements of this title" of the second half of the sentence. Nevertheless, many courts—including the Supreme Court—have turned the term "useful" of this phrase into the "utility" requirement for the patentability of an invention.

Case Law

The following section includes several summaries of court cases addressing the utility requirement. As shown by the following cases, while the utility requirement was a significant hurdle for some inventions in the past, it is now a relatively easy hurdle for most inventions.

In *Brennar v. Manson*, Manson invented a process for a steroid. The patent application claimed a new process for making the steroid, but the detailed description did not disclose any particular use for the steroid. A steroid that was chemically related to the Manson steroid was proven to inhibit tumors in mice. The effects of chemically related steroids on humans are not, however, predictable from their effects on mice. The USPTO, under Commissioner Brennar, rejected the claims on the process for the steroid as not having a use and, therefore, not useful under 35 U.S.C. 101. The Supreme Court held that an application on a process that produces a known product must include the usefulness of the product to satisfy the utility requirement under 35 U.S.C. 101. The Court stated that "[A] patent is not a hunting license. It is not a reward for the search, but compensation for its successful conclusion" See *Brennar v. Manson* (1966).

Comment

The USPTO and the courts have relaxed their position on the *Brennar* case during the past few decades. Now, animal testing can generally satisfy utility for pharmaceutical products. The dissent in the *Brenner* case, especially when an intermediate product is marketable to scientists for research purposes, is now the preferred view.

In the *Juicy Whip, Inc. v. Orange Bang, Inc.* case, the Federal Circuit stated, "The fact that one product can be altered to make it look like another is in itself a specific benefit sufficient to satisfy the statutory requirements of utility." See *Juicy Whip,*

Inc. v. Orange Bang, Inc. (Fed. Cir. 1999). The Juicy Whip case overturned a long history of cases that struck down patents because the use of the invention was simply to imitate something else. Now devices or systems that imitate another system satisfy the utility requirement. Machines that merely amuse or entertain also satisfy the utility requirement. Further still, as held in *Whistler Corp. v. Autotronics, Inc.*, radar detectors—despite the fact that their only use is to circumvent the law—can satisfy the utility requirement of 35 U.S.C. 101. See *Whistler Corp. v. Autotronics, Inc.* (N.D. Tex. 1988).

Novelty Requirement

Introduction and Statute

The novelty requirement functions to filter out patent applications on inventions that are already disclosed to the public. The relevant statutory language regarding the novelty requirement appears below:

A person shall be entitled to a patent unless—

(1) the claimed invention was patented, described in a printed publication, or in public use, on sale, or otherwise available to the public before the effective filing date of the claimed invention; or

(2) the claimed invention was described in a patent issued ... or in an application for patent published ... in which the patent or application, as the case may be, names another inventor and was effectively filed before the effective filing date of the claimed invention.

The knowledge that can be proved as being known or used by others in this country or that can proved as disclosed in a printed publication (e.g., a published application, an issued patent, a published thesis, a journal article, or even a website) is referred to as "prior art." A claim of a patent application fails the novelty requirement if the invention was described in a single occurrence of the prior art.

Tips for Understanding the Novelty Requirement

In the below image, assume that the pattern of the circle on the left represents the limitations of a claim and the pattern on the six circles on the right represents the individual disclosures of the prior art. Is the claim novel over the prior art?

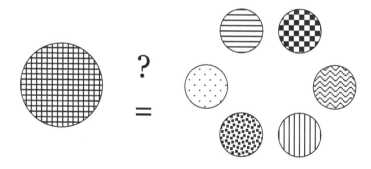

The specific pattern of the circle on the left is not taught from a single occurrence of the patterns on the six circles on the right. Therefore, claim would be novel over this prior art.

Case Law

In *Rosaire v. National Lead Co.*, Rosaire alleges to have invented a new method for finding oil in 1936. National Lead contends that a third party knew and extensively used the same method in the fields without any deliberate attempt at concealment before 1936. The court held that an invention that was used by a third party, even though not patented or published by the third party, is not novel under 35 U.S.C. 102a. See *Rosaire v. National Lead Co.* (5th Cir. 1955).

Non-Obviousness Requirement

Introduction and Statute

As stated by the Supreme Court, "The inherent problem [of the patent system] was to develop some means of weeding out those inventions which would not be disclosed or devised but for the inducement of a patent" *Graham v. John Deere Co.* (Supreme Court 1966). The novelty requirement weeded out the patent applications on inventions that were already disclosed to the public. But what about the patent applications on inventions that were obvious changes to the inventions already disclosed to the public? The relevant statutory language regarding the non-obviousness requirement appears below:

"A patent may not be obtained... if the differences between the subject matter sought to be patented and the prior art are such that the subject matter as a whole would have been obvious at the time the invention was made to a person having ordinary skill in the art to which said subject matter pertains" (35 U.S.C. 103a).

The obviousness requirement specifically states "at the time the invention was made." Many elegant inventions appear incredibly simple or quite obvious once the inventions are described. While the patent laws prohibit this type of analysis, it is often difficult (or impossible!) difficult to avoid this bias.

35 U.S.C. §103 (and thus the non-obviousness requirement) state that the invention is obvious if "the subject matter ... would have been obvious ... to a person having ordinary skill in the art to which said subject matter pertains." The person having ordinary skill in the art is a mythical person with a predetermined level of skill that has been deemed "ordinary." It is a common misconception that the level of skill of the inventor is the "ordinary" skill in the art. This is not always the case. Rather, the "ordinary" skill should be of the level of skill of the average skilled worker in this art or technology. This is generally at the level of a college degree; however, depending on the art, a PhD may be "ordinary."

Tips for Understanding the Non-Obviousness Requirement

A claim of a patent application fails the non-obviousness requirement if the invention is merely an obvious combination of the prior art. In the below image, again assume that the pattern of the circle on the left represents the limitations of a claim and the pattern on the six circles on the right represents the individual disclosures of the prior art. Is the claim novel obvious in light of the prior art?

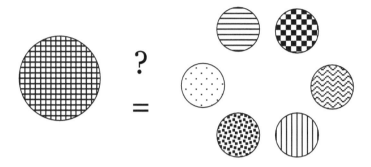

One might argue that the cross-hatch pattern is simply an overlay of a horizontal pattern and a vertical pattern, which are both taught in the prior art. If this argument prevails, the invention would not be patentable because it would be an obvious combination of the prior art. One could argue, however, that nothing in the prior art teaches the crossing of lines and that this crossing of lines is obvious only in hindsight. If this argument prevails, the invention would be patentable because it is not an obvious combination of the prior art.

The novelty requirement is fairly objective, while the non-obviousness requirement is fairly subjective. For this reason, there are few patent law cases that deal directly with novelty; nearly all patent law cases deal with obviousness.

Case Law

35 U.S.C. 103 codified the third major requirement to the patent statutes (along with proper subject matter and novelty). As interpreted under the following *Graham* case, Section 103 requires an "inventive leap" from the prior art to a patentable

invention, which counterbalances the strong rights given to patent owners.

Graham v. John Deere Co. (Supreme Court 1966)

MR. JUSTICE CLARK delivered the opinion of the Court:

I.

Graham v. *John Deere Co.*, an infringement suit by petitioners, presents a conflict between two Circuits over the validity of a single patent on a "Clamp for vibrating Shank Plows." The invention, a combination of old mechanical elements, involves a device designed to absorb shock from plow shanks as they plow through rocky soil and thus to prevent damage to the plow. In 1955, the Fifth Circuit had held the patent valid under its rule that when a combination produces an "old result in a cheaper and otherwise more advantageous way," it is patentable. In 1964, the Eighth Circuit held that there was no new result in the patented combination and that the patent was, therefore, not valid. Although we have determined that neither Circuit applied the correct test, we conclude that the patent is invalid under §103 and, therefore, we affirm the judgment of the Eighth Circuit.

II.

At the outset it must be remembered that the federal patent power stems from a specific constitutional provision, which authorizes the Congress "To promote the Progress of ... useful Arts, by securing for limited Times to ... Inventors the exclusive Right to their ... Discoveries." The clause is both a grant of power and a limitation. This qualified authority, unlike the power often exercised in the sixteenth and seventeenth centuries by the English Crown, is limited to the promotion of advances in the "useful arts." It was written against the backdrop of the practices —eventually curtailed by the Statute of Monopolies—of the Crown in granting monopolies to court favorites in goods or businesses which had long before been enjoyed by the public. The Congress in the exercise of the patent power may not overreach the restraints imposed by the stated constitutional purpose. Nor may it enlarge the patent monopoly without regard to the innovation, advancement or social benefit gained thereby. Moreover, Congress may not authorize the issuance of patents whose effects are to remove existent knowledge from the public domain, or to restrict free access to materials already available. Innovation, advancement, and things which add to the sum of useful knowledge are inherent requisites in a patent system which by constitutional command must "promote the Progress of . . . useful Arts." This is the *standard* expressed in the Constitution and it may not be ignored. And it is in this light that patent validity "requires reference to a standard written into the Constitution."

Congress quickly responded to the bidding of the Constitution by enacting the Patent Act of 1790 during the second session of the First Congress. It created an agency in the Department of State headed by the Secretary of State, the Secretary of the Department of War and the Attorney General, any two of whom could issue a patent for a period not exceeding 14 years to any petitioner that "hath ... invented or discovered any useful art, manufacture, ... or device, or any improvement therein not before known or used" if the board found that "the invention or discovery [was] sufficiently useful and important...." 1 Stat. 110. This group, whose members administered the patent system along with their other public duties, was known by its own designation as "Commissioners for the Promotion of Useful Arts."

Thomas Jefferson, who as Secretary of State was a member of the group, was its moving spirit and might well be called the "first administrator of our patent system." He was not only an administrator of the patent system under the 1790 Act, but was also the author of the 1793 Patent Act. In addition, Jefferson was himself an inventor of great note. His unpatented improvements on plows, to mention but one line of his inventions, won acclaim and recognition on both sides of the Atlantic. Because of his active interest and influence in the early development of the patent system, Jefferson's views on the general nature of the limited patent monopoly under the Constitution, as well as his conclusions as to conditions for patentability under the statutory scheme, are worthy of note.

Jefferson's philosophy on the nature and purpose of the patent monopoly is expressed in a letter to Isaac McPherson (Aug. 1813). He rejected a natural-rights theory in intellectual property rights and clearly recognized the social and economic rationale of the patent system. The patent monopoly was not designed to secure to the inventor his natural right in his discoveries. Rather, it was a reward, an inducement, to bring forth new knowledge. The grant of an exclusive right to an invention was the creation of society—at odds with the inherent free nature of disclosed ideas—and was not to be freely given. Only inventions and discoveries which furthered human knowledge, and were new and useful, justified the special inducement of a limited private monopoly. Jefferson did not believe in granting patents for small details, obvious improvements, or frivolous devices. His writings evidence his insistence upon a high level of patentability.

III.

The difficulty of formulating conditions for patentability was heightened by the generality of the constitutional grant and the statutes implementing it, together with the underlying policy of the patent system that "the things which are worth to the public the embarrassment of an exclusive patent," as Jefferson put it, must outweigh the restrictive effect of the limited patent monopoly. The inherent problem was to develop some means of weeding out those inventions which would not be disclosed or devised but for the inducement of a patent.

This Court formulated a general condition of patentability in 1851 in *Hotchkiss v. Greenwood, 11 How. 248*. The patent involved a mere substitution of materials—porcelain or clay for wood or metal in doorknobs—and the Court condemned it, holding: "Unless more ingenuity and skill . . . were required . . . than were possessed by an ordinary mechanic acquainted with the business, there was an absence of that degree of skill and ingenuity which constitute essential elements of every invention. In other words, the improvement is the work of the skilful mechanic, not that of the inventor."

Hotchkiss, by positing the condition that a patentable invention evidence more ingenuity and skill than that possessed by an ordinary mechanic acquainted with the business, merely distinguished between new and useful innovations that were capable of sustaining a patent and those that were not. The *Hotchkiss* test laid the cornerstone of the judicial evolution suggested by Jefferson and left to the courts by Congress. In practice, *Hotchkiss* has required a comparison between the subject matter of the patent, or patent application, and the background skill of the calling. It has been from this comparison that patentability was in each case determined.

...

V.

Under § 103, the scope and content of the prior art are to be determined; differences between the prior art and the claims at issue are to be ascertained; and the level of ordinary skill in the pertinent art resolved. Against this background, the obviousness or nonobviousness of the subject matter is determined. Such secondary considerations as commercial success, long felt but unsolved needs, failure of others, etc., might be utilized to give light to the circumstances surrounding the origin of the subject matter sought to be patented. As indicia of obviousness or nonobviousness, these inquiries may have relevancy.

This is not to say, however, that there will not be difficulties in applying the nonobviousness test. What is obvious is not a question upon which there is likely to be uniformity of thought in every given factual context. The difficulties, however, are comparable to those encountered daily by the courts in such frames of reference as negligence and scienter, and should be amenable to a case-by-case development. We believe that strict observance of the requirements laid down here will result in that uniformity and definiteness which Congress called for in the 1952 Act.

While we have focused attention on the appropriate standard to be applied by the courts, it must be remembered that the primary responsibility for sifting out unpatentable material lies in the Patent Office. To await litigation is—for all practical purposes—to debilitate the patent system. We have observed a notorious difference between the standards applied by the Patent Office and by the courts. While many reasons can be adduced to explain the discrepancy, one may well be the free rein often exercised by Examiners in their use of the concept of "invention." In this connection we note that the Patent Office is confronted with a most difficult task. Almost 100,000 applications for patents are filed each year. Of these, about 50,000 are granted and the backlog now runs well over 200,000. 1965 Annual Report of the Commissioner of Patents 13-14. This is itself a compelling reason for the Commissioner to strictly adhere to the 1952 Act as interpreted here. This would, we believe, not only expedite disposition but bring about a closer concurrence between administrative and judicial precedent.

Although we conclude here that the inquiry which the Patent Office and the courts must make as to patentability must be beamed with greater intensity on the requirements of §103, it bears repeating that we find no change in the general strictness with which the overall test is to be applied. We have been urged to find in § 103 a relaxed standard, supposedly a congressional reaction to the "increased standard" applied by this Court in its decisions over the last 20 or 30 years. The standard has remained invariable in this Court. Technology, however, has advanced—and with remarkable rapidity in the last 50 years. Moreover, the ambit of applicable art in given fields of science has widened by disciplines unheard of a half century ago. It is but an evenhanded application to require that those persons granted the benefit of a patent monopoly be charged with an awareness of these changed conditions. The same is true of the less technical, but still useful arts. He who seeks to build a better mousetrap today has a long path to tread before reaching the Patent Office.

VI.

The Patent in Issue in No. 11, Graham *v.* John Deere Co.

This patent, No. 2,627,798 (hereinafter called the '798 patent) relates to a spring clamp which permits plow shanks to be pushed upward when they hit obstructions in the soil, and then springs the shanks back into normal position when the obstruction is passed over. The device, which we show diagrammatically in the [below] sketch, is fixed to the plow frame as a unit.

The mechanism around which the controversy centers is basically a hinge. The top half of it, known as the upper plate, is a heavy metal piece clamped to the plow frame and is stationary relative to the plow frame. The lower half of the hinge, known as the hinge plate, is connected to the rear of the upper plate by a hinge pin and rotates downward with respect to it. The shank, which is bolted to the forward end of the hinge plate, runs beneath the plate and parallel to it for about nine inches, passes through a stirrup, and then continues backward for several feet curving down toward the ground. The chisel, which does the actual plowing, is attached to the rear end of the shank. As the plow frame is pulled forward, the chisel rips through the soil, thereby plowing it. In the normal position, the hinge plate and the shank are kept tight against the upper plate by a spring, which is atop the upper plate. A rod runs through the center of the spring, extending down through holes in both plates and the shank. Its upper end is bolted to the top of the spring while its lower end is hooked against the underside of the shank.

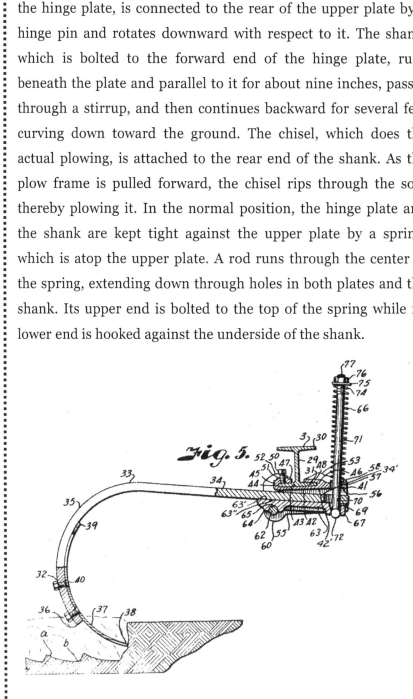

When the chisel hits a rock or other obstruction in the soil, the obstruction forces the chisel and the rear portion of the shank to move upward. The shank is pivoted against the rear of the hinge plate and pries open the hinge against the closing tendency of the spring. This closing tendency is caused by the fact that, as the hinge is opened, the connecting rod is pulled downward and the spring is compressed. When the obstruction is passed over, the upward force on the chisel disappears and the spring pulls the shank and hinge plate back into their original position. The lower, rear portion of the hinge plate is constructed in the form of a stirrup which brackets the shank, passing around and beneath it. The shank fits loosely into the stirrup (permitting a slight up and down play). The stirrup is designed to prevent the shank from recoiling away from the hinge plate, and thus prevents excessive strain on the shank near its bolted connection. The stirrup also girds the shank, preventing it from fishtailing from side to side.

In practical use, a number of spring-hinge-shank combinations are clamped to a plow frame, forming a set of ground-working chisels capable of withstanding the shock of rocks and other obstructions in the soil without breaking the shanks.

Background of the Patent.
Chisel plows, as they are called, were developed for plowing in areas where the ground is relatively free from rocks or stones. Originally, the shanks were rigidly attached to the plow frames. When such plows were used in the rocky, glacial soils of some of the Northern States, they were found to have serious defects. As

the chisels hit buried rocks, a vibratory motion was set up and tremendous forces were transmitted to the shank near its connection to the frame. The shanks would break. Graham, one of the petitioners, sought to meet that problem, and in 1950 obtained a patent, U.S. No. *2,493,811* (hereinafter *'811*), on a spring clamp which solved some of the difficulties. Graham and his companies manufactured and sold the *'811* clamps. In 1950, Graham modified the *'811* structure and filed for a patent. That patent, the one in issue, was granted in 1953. This suit against competing plow manufacturers resulted from charges by petitioners that several of respondents' devices infringed the '798 patent.

The Prior Art.

Five prior patents indicating the state of the art were cited by the Patent Office in the prosecution of the '798 application. Four of these patents, 10 other United States patents and two prior-use spring-clamp arrangements not of record in the '798 file wrapper were relied upon by respondents as revealing the prior art. The District Court and the Court of Appeals found that the prior art "as a whole in one form or another contains all of the mechanical elements of the 798 Patent." One of the prior-use clamp devices not before the Patent Examiner—Glencoe—was found to have "all of the elements."

We confine our discussion to the prior patent of Graham, *'811*, and to the Glencoe clamp device, both among the references asserted by respondents. The Graham *'811* and '798 patent devices are similar in all elements, save two: (1) the stirrup and the bolted connection of the shank to the hinge plate do not appear in '811; and (2) the position of the shank is reversed, being placed in patent '811 above the hinge plate, sandwiched between it and the upper plate. The shank is held in place by the spring rod which is hooked against the bottom of the hinge plate passing through a slot in the shank. Other differences are of no consequence to our examination. In practice the '811 patent arrangement permitted the shank to wobble or fishtail because it was not rigidly fixed to the hinge plate; moreover, as the hinge plate was below the shank, the latter caused wear on the upper plate, a member difficult to repair or replace.

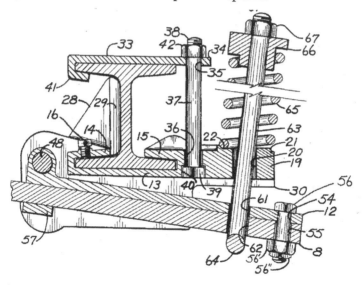

Graham's '798 patent application contained 12 claims. All were rejected as not distinguished from the Graham '811 patent. The inverted position of the shank was specifically rejected as was the bolting of the shank to the hinge plate. The Patent Office examiner found these to be "matters of design well within the expected skill of the art and devoid of invention." Graham withdrew the original claims and substituted the two new ones which are substantially those in issue here. His contention was that wear was reduced in patent '798 between the shank and the heel or rear of the upper plate.* He also emphasized several new features, the relevant one here being that the bolt used to connect the hinge plate and shank maintained the upper face of the shank in continuing and constant contact with the underface of the hinge plate.

> * In '811, where the shank was above the hinge plate, an upward movement of the chisel forced the shank up against the underside of the rear of the upper plate. The upper plate thus provided the fulcrum about which the hinge was pried open. Because of this, as well as the location of the hinge pin, the shank rubbed against the heel of the upper plate causing wear both to the plate and to the shank. By relocating the hinge pin and by placing the hinge plate between the shank and the upper plate, as in '798, the rubbing was eliminated and the wear point was changed to the hinge plate, a member more easily removed or replaced for repair.

Graham did not urge before the Patent Office the greater "flexing" qualities of the '798 patent arrangement which he so heavily relied on in the courts. The sole element in patent '798 which petitioners argue before us is the interchanging of the shank and hinge plate and the consequences flowing from this arrangement. The contention is that this arrangement—which petitioners claim is not disclosed in the prior art—permits the shank to flex under stress for its *entire* length. As we have sketched (see sketch, "Graham '798 Patent" in Appendix, Fig. 2), when the chisel hits an obstruction the resultant force (A) pushes the rear of the shank upward and the shank pivots against the rear of the hinge plate at (C). The natural tendency is for that portion of the shank between the pivot point and the bolted connection (*i.e.*, between C and D) to bow downward and away from the hinge plate. The maximum distance (B) that the shank moves away from the plate is slight—for emphasis, greatly exaggerated in the sketches. This is so because of the strength of the shank and the short—nine inches or so—length of that portion of the shank between (C) and (D). On the contrary, in patent '811 (see sketch, "Graham '811 Patent" in Appendix, Fig. 2), the pivot point is the upper plate at point (c); and while the tendency for the shank to bow between points (c) and (d) is the same as in '798, the shank is restricted because of the underlying hinge plate and cannot flex as freely. In practical effect, the shank flexes only between points (a) and (c), and not along the entire length of the shank, as in '798. Petitioners say that this difference in flex, though small, effectively absorbs the tremendous forces of the shock of obstructions whereas prior art arrangements failed.

The Obviousness of the Differences.

We cannot agree with petitioners. We assume that the prior art does not disclose such an arrangement as petitioners claim in patent '798. Still we do not believe that the argument on which petitioners' contention is bottomed supports the validity of the patent. The tendency of the shank to flex is the same in all cases. If free-flexing, as petitioners now argue, is the crucial difference above the prior art, then it appears evident that the desired result would be obtainable by not boxing the shank within the confines of the hinge. The only other effective place available in the arrangement was to attach it below the hinge plate and run it through a stirrup or bracket that would not disturb its flexing qualities. Certainly a person having ordinary skill in the prior art, given the fact that the flex in the shank could be utilized more effectively if allowed to run the entire length of the shank, would immediately see that the thing to do was what Graham did, *i.e.*, invert the shank and the hinge plate.

Petitioners' argument basing validity on the free-flex theory raised for the first time on appeal is reminiscent of *Lincoln Engineering Co. v. Stewart-Warner Corp., 303 U.S. 545 (1938)*, where the Court called such an effort "an afterthought. No such function . . . is hinted at in the specifications of the patent. If this were so vital an element in the functioning of the apparatus it is strange that all mention of it was omitted." At p. 550. No "flexing" argument was raised in the Patent Office. Indeed, the trial judge specifically found that "flexing is not a claim of the patent in suit . . ." and would not permit interrogation as to flexing in the accused devices. Moreover, the clear testimony of petitioners' experts shows that the flexing advantages flowing from the '798 arrangement are not, in fact, a significant feature in the patent.

We find no nonobvious facets in the '798 arrangement. The wear and repair claims were sufficient to overcome the patent examiner's original conclusions as to the validity of the patent. However, some of the prior art, notably Glencoe, was not before him. There the hinge plate is below the shank but, as the courts below found, all of the elements in the '798 patent are present in the Glencoe structure. Furthermore, even though the position of the shank and hinge plate appears reversed in Glencoe, the mechanical operation is identical. The shank there pivots about the underside of the stirrup, which in Glencoe is *above* the shank. In other words, the stirrup in Glencoe serves exactly the same function as the heel of the hinge plate in '798. The mere shifting of the wear point to the heel of the '798 hinge plate from the stirrup of Glencoe—itself a part of the hinge plate—presents no operative mechanical distinctions, much less nonobvious differences.

The judgment of the Court of Appeals in No. 11 is affirmed.
It is so ordered.

Does non-obvious = difficult?

If a person having ordinary skill in the art would have been able to pose the problem, find the solution, and foresee the result, the inventive step is lacking. Sometimes, like the situation for the Amazon "one-click patent," the solution lacks an inventive step and the results are not surprising. The framing or identifying of the problem was the inventive step. In the situation for the one-click patent, everyone was stuck in the shopping cart metaphor, which had the disadvantage of "abandoned shopping carts." The one-click patent reframed the problem.

Teaching, Suggestion, or Motivation

In an attempt to make the obviousness test less subjective, the Court of Appeals for the Federal Circuit stated that "[A] proper analysis under section 103 requires... consideration of two factors: (1) whether the prior art would have suggested to those of ordinary skill in the art that they should make the claimed [invention]; and (2) whether... those of ordinary skill would have a reasonable expectation of success." See *In re Vaeck* (Fed. Cir. 1991). For several years, this teaching, suggestion, or motivation (i.e., TSM) was the only method to determine obviousness. In the recent *KSR International Co. v. Teleflex, Inc.,* the Supreme Court stated that TSM is only one method of finding obviousness and that, returning to the *Graham* test, "the scope and content of the prior art are to be determined; differences between the prior art and the claims at issue are to be ascertained; and the level of ordinary skill in the pertinent art resolved. Against this background, the... nonobviousness of the subject matter is determined." See *KSR International Co. v. Teleflex, Inc.* (2007). While the media hailed this as an "abrupt change" and declared this as making "thousands of patents worthless," patent practitioners considered it as a mild readjustment to the seminal Supreme Court decision.

Secondary Considerations

In *Graham v. John Deere Co.,* the Supreme Court stated that "Such secondary considerations as commercial success, long felt but unsolved needs, failure of others, etc., might be utilized to give light to the circumstances surrounding the origin of the subject matter sought to be patented. As indicia of obviousness or nonobviousness, these inquiries may have relevancy." Thus, an obviousness rejection (under 35 U.S.C. 103) can potentially be overcome by filing an affidavit under 37 CFR 1.132 and declaring that:

- The invention had unexpected properties,
- The products or methods using the invention had commercial success, or
- The invention solved a long-standing problem in the field.

Overcoming obviousness

An obviousness rejection (under 35 U.S.C. 103) may be overcome by:

- Arguing that the combination of the references does not teach or disclose every element of the rejected claim,
- Arguing that none of the references provide any motivation for the combination (or that a reference actually teaches away from the combination),
- Providing evidence of secondary considerations (of the *Graham* case),
- Amending the rejected claim to include an element not taught by the combination.

How to Conduct a Patentability Search

Introduction

As discussed above, for an invention to be patentable, it must be both novel and not obvious over past inventions (i.e., what has already been done). Considering the costs to prepare and file a patent application, it is often appropriate to conduct a patentability search to identify the prior art and to consequently determine the corresponding availability and scope of a patent application based on the invention in question.

The USPTO provides a free search engine on their website (http://www.uspto.gov), which is split into two databases: issued patents and published applications. The search engine provides two primary search tools: Keyword search and Classification search. There are at least four secondary search tools: Backward and Forward Citation searches, as well as Inventor and Assignee searches.

Primary Search Tools

Keyword search is simply a text search engine based on Boolean logic ("AND", "NOT", etc.). While most of today's society is comfortable with text search engines (e.g., a typical Google search), there is an inherent problem with text searches for prior art within the patent database: patent applications are nearly always filed before the technology is commercialized and a common vernacular has been established. An attempt, for example, to search for the original patent on the microwave oven will not succeed. The title of U.S. Patent No. 2,495,429 is "Method of Treating Foodstuffs" and the phrase "microwave oven" does not appear in the entire patent. For this reason, the USPTO examiners and the professional prior art searchers use a combination of keyword searches and classification searches.

The classification system at the Patent Office is similar to the Dewey Decimal System for books and texts in many libraries.

Every issued patent and published application is classified according to the structure and/or function of the disclosure of the patent document. There are about 450 Classes of invention and about 150,000 subclasses. Searching the classifications overcomes the inherent problem of text searches, but often produces too many prior art references to be reviewed. For this reason, an optimum search strategy often combines elements of text search and a classification search.

Secondary Search Tools

Within every issued patent, the electronic version of the patent document at the www.USPTO.gov website lists the patents that were cited during the prosecution of the patent under the phrase "References Cited." Searching these patents is known as a Backward Citation. Typically, if the issued patent is relevant, the cited references are relevant.

Within every issued patent, the USPTO also includes a link, under the phrase "Referenced By," to jump to the future patents that cite or reference back to the issued patent. Searching these patents is known as Forward Citation. Again, if the issued patent is relevant, the references that cite the issued patent are typically relevant.

In some situations, searching for more issued patents that were invented by a particular inventor may be useful. In other situations, searching for more issued patents that were assigned to a particular company may be useful. Keep in mind, however, that many companies have affiliations with completely different names. For example, the Minnesota Mining and Manufacturing Company has affiliations that use the abbreviation 3M. Also, some companies share part of their name (e.g., Apple Computer Inc. and Apple Medical Corporation).

Recommended Search Strategy

The best searches use an iterative approach, which is outlined below:

- Conduct a Keyword Search. If the search provides more than 200 results, refine by searching only within the abstracts of the Issued Patents (with the "ABST/" option). Once a search provides approximately 200 results, review the patents and record the classifications of the most relevant Issued Patents.

- Conduct a Classification Search. Using the Classification Manual (http://www.uspto.gov/go/classification), review the Class Definitions of the three most relevant Classes as determined by the Keyword Search performed as described above. If the Classes are still relevant to the search, review the Class Schedule for each relevant Class. Either click on the "A" for a list of all Issued Patents referenced and cross-referenced within the entire Class, or click on a "P" for a list within a certain Subclass. Click on the subclass for a definition. The dot system, used in the Class Schedule, is shorthand for an outline.

- Conduct a combination Keyword and Classification Search. Skim the Abstract and/or drawings of at least 200 prior art references.

- Conduct a Forward and Backward Search of the most relevant patents and, if appropriate, an Assignee and/or Inventor search.
- Review the most relevant patents for more relevant keywords and classifications.
- Repeat the process until the same patent documents continue to appear. To approach a comprehensive search, approximately 500 prior art references should be at least skimmed.
- Since the issued patent and published application databases are separately accessed by the search engine at the USPTO, repeat the best search query within the published application database.

Chapter Five

When Should the Patent Application be Filed?

"It is a condition upon an inventor's right to a patent that he shall not exploit his discovery competitively after it is ready for patenting; he must content himself with either secrecy, or legal monopoly."—Judge Learned Hand (*Metallizing Eng'g Co., Inc., v. Kenyon Bearing & Auto Parts Co.,* Inc., 153 F.2d 516, 520 (2d Cir. 1946))

Chapter Contents

- Introduction
- Timing Requirement
    - Introduction
    - Statute
    - What Is a Printed Publication?
    - What Is a Public Use?
    - What Is an Offer for Sale?
    - Foreign Filing Considerations
- How to Prepare and File a Provisional Application
    - Introduction
    - Written Description
    - Drawings
    - Filing Fee
    - Cover Sheet or Application Data Sheet
    - Submission of the Provisional Application

Introduction

The discussion in this chapter addresses the importance of establishing a priority date. A priority date is the date granted by the USPTO to the applicant upon receipt of a provisional application or a patent application that includes any required drawings, a specification, and—if the application is a patent application and not a provisional application—at least one claim. Additional patent applications that are filed after the original application (e.g., a patent application filed after a provisional application or a continuation application filed after a patent application) may assert priority back to the original application and therefore be granted the same priority date (e.g., same effective filing date) as the original application. The priority date serves to "trump" or disqualify other patent applications that were filed after the priority date.

To establish a priority date the applicant must meet the first-inventor-to-file requirement and timing requirement, as well as submit either a provisional application or a patent application that meets the written description requirement. The discussion in this Chapter will address these requirements and will conclude with some high-level instructions on how to prepare and file a provisional application.

Switch from First-to-Invent to First-Inventor-to-File
All patent applications filed before March 16th, 2013 are examined under the old first-to-invent patent system, while all

patent applications filed on or after March 16th, 2013 are examined under the new first-inventor-to-file patent system.

Under the old system, if a claim of a pending patent application is rejected by the USPTO as not being novel (under the previous 35 U.S.C. §102a or §102e statutes) in light of a particular printed publication, published application, or issued patent, the inventor has—in certain situations—an opportunity to overcome the novelty rejection by providing proof that the invention date of his or her invention occurred before the invention date of the printed publication or issued patent. To determine the first-to-invent between the two inventors, one must consider the *conception date*, the *reduction to practice date*, and the *reasonable diligence* of each of the two inventors. This is a complex determination, which is typically reserved for interference proceedings and infringement lawsuits. In these situations, a bound and dated notebook to chronicle the conception and reduction to practice of the invention is often very useful.

Timing Requirement

Introduction

In the United States, inventors are allowed to describe their invention in a printed publication, publicly use their invention, and offer their invention for sale before filing a U.S. patent application. However, these three events start the clock running; the inventor must file a patent application on the invention within 1 year or lose all rights to obtain a patent on the invention. This 1 year period is referred to as a "grace period."

Statute

A disclosure made 1 year or less before the effective filing date of a claimed invention shall not be prior art to the claimed invention ... if—

(A) the disclosure was made by the inventor or joint inventor or by another who obtained the subject matter disclosed directly or indirectly from the inventor or a joint inventor; or

(B) the subject matter disclosed had, before such disclosure, been publicly disclosed by the inventor or a joint inventor or another who obtained the subject matter disclosed directly or indirectly from the inventor or a joint inventor. (35 U.S.C. 102b).

What Is a Printed Publication?

The interpretation of the phrase *printed publication* originally meant only books or other documents prepared in a printing press. Recently, the phrase printed publication has been interpreted as "public accessibility." *According to In re Hall* (Fed. Cir. 1986), a single copy of a doctorial thesis, which was properly cataloged in a foreign university library, was a printed publication. In contrast, according to *In re Cronyn* (Fed. Cir. 1989), three undergraduate theses deposited in a college library are not printed publications if they are not appropriately indexed. An HTML document, indexed by the Google search engine, is generally considered a printed publication.

The following section includes an excerpt from the 2004 Federal Circuit case of *In Re Klopfenstein* that lists the factors that determine "public accessibility" and determine if a reference can be considered a printed publication.

In Re Klopfenstein (Fed. Cir. 2004)

Circuit Judge Prost authored the following opinion:

Carol Klopfenstein and John Brent appeal a decision from the Patent and Trademark Office's Board of Patent Appeals and Interferences ("Board") upholding the denial of their patent application. The Board upheld the Patent and Trademark Office's ("PTO's") initial denial of their application on the ground that the invention described in the patent application was not novel under 35 U.S.C. § 102(b) because it had already been described in a printed publication more than one year before the date of the patent application. We affirm.

BACKGROUND

The appellants applied for a patent on October 30, 2000. Their patent application, Patent Application Serial No. 09/699,950 ("the '950 application"), discloses methods of preparing foods comprising extruded soy cotyledon fiber ("SCF"). The '950 application asserts that feeding mammals foods containing extruded SCF may help lower their serum cholesterol levels while raising HDL cholesterol levels. The fact that extrusion reduces cholesterol levels was already known by those of ordinary skill in the art that worked with SCF. What was not known at the time was that double extrusion increases this effect and yielded even stronger results.

In October 1998, the appellants, along with colleague M. Liu, presented a printed slide presentation ("Liu" or "the Liu reference") entitled "Enhancement of Cholesterol-Lowering Activity of Dietary Fibers By Extrusion Processing" at a meeting of the American Association of Cereal Chemists ("AACC"). The fourteen-slide presentation was printed and pasted onto poster boards. The printed slide presentation was displayed continuously for two and a half days at the AACC meeting. In November of that same year, the same slide presentation was put on display for less than a day at an Agriculture Experiment Station ("AES") at Kansas State University.

Both parties agree that the Liu reference presented to the AACC and at the AES in 1998 disclosed every limitation of the invention disclosed in the '950 patent application. Furthermore, at neither presentation was there a disclaimer or notice to the intended audience prohibiting note-taking or copying of the presentation. Finally, no copies of the presentation were disseminated either at the AACC meeting or at the AES, and the presentation was never catalogued or indexed in any library or database.

On October 24, 2001, nearly one year after its filing, the '950 patent application was rejected by the PTO examiner. The examiner found all of the application's claims anticipated by the Liu reference or obvious in view of Liu and other references. The appellants argued that the Liu reference was not a "printed publication" because no copies were distributed and because there was no evidence that the reference was photographed. The examiner rejected these arguments and issued a final office action on April 10, 2002 rejecting the claims of the '950 application.

DISCUSSION

The only question in this appeal is whether the Liu reference constitutes a "printed publication" for the purposes of 35 U.S.C. § 102(b). The appellants argue on appeal that the key to establishing whether or not a reference constitutes a "printed publication" lies in determining whether or not it had been disseminated by the distribution of reproductions or copies and/or indexed in a library or database. They assert that because the Liu reference was not distributed and indexed, it cannot count as a "printed publication" for the purposes of 35 U.S.C. § 102(b). To support their argument, they rely on several precedents from this court and our predecessor court on "printed publications." They argue that *In re Cronyn*, *In re Hall*, and *In re Wyer*, among other cases, all support the view that distribution and/or indexing is required for something to be considered a "printed publication."

We find the appellants' argument unconvincing and disagree with their characterization of our controlling precedent. Even if the cases cited by the appellants relied on inquiries into distribution and indexing to reach their holdings, they do not limit this court to finding something to be a "printed publication" only when there is distribution and/or indexing. Indeed, the key inquiry is whether or not a reference has been made "publicly accessible." As we have previously stated,

> The statutory phrase "printed publication" has been interpreted to mean that before the critical date the reference must have been sufficiently accessible to the public interested in the art; dissemination and public accessibility are the keys to the legal determination whether a prior art reference was "published."

In re Cronyn, 890 F.2d at 1160. For example, a public billboard targeted to those of ordinary skill in the art that describes all of the limitations of an invention and that is on display for the public for months may be neither "distributed" nor "indexed"— but it most surely is "sufficiently accessible to the public interested in the art" and therefore, under controlling precedent, a "printed publication." Thus, the appellants' argument that "distribution and/or indexing" are the key components to a "printed publication" inquiry fails to properly reflect what our precedent stands for.

Furthermore, the cases that the appellants rely on can be clearly distinguished from this case. *Cronyn* involved college students' presentations of their undergraduate theses to a defense committee made up of four faculty members. Their theses were later catalogued in an index in the college's main library. The index was made up of thousands of individual cards that contained only a student's name and the title of his or her thesis. The index was searchable by student name and the actual theses themselves were neither included in the index nor made publicly accessible. We held that because the theses were only presented to a handful of faculty members and "had not been cataloged [sic] or indexed in a meaningful way," they were not sufficiently publicly accessible for the purposes of 35 U.S.C. § 102(b). *In re Cronyn*, 890 F.2d at 1161.

In *Hall*, this court determined that a thesis filed and indexed in a university library did count as a "printed publication." The *Hall* court arrived at its holding after taking into account that copies of the indexed thesis itself were made freely available to the general public by the university more than one year before the filing of the relevant patent application in that case. But the court in *Hall* did not rest its holding merely on the indexing of the thesis in question. Instead, it used indexing as a factor in determining "public accessibility." As the court asserted:

> The ["printed publication"] bar is grounded on the principle that once an invention is in the public domain, it is no longer patentable by anyone. . . . Because there are many ways in which a reference may be disseminated to the interested public, "public accessibility" has been called the touchstone in determining whether a reference constitutes a "printed publication" bar under 35 U.S.C. § 102(b).

In re Hall, 781 F.2d at 898-99.

Finally, the *Wyer* court determined that an Australian patent application kept on microfilm at the Australian Patent Office was "sufficiently accessible to the public and to persons skilled in the pertinent art to qualify as a 'printed publication.'" The court so found even though it did not determine whether or not there was "actual viewing or dissemination" of the patent application. It was sufficient for the court's purposes that the records of the application were kept so that they could be accessible to the public. According to the *Wyer* court, the entire purpose of the "printed publication" bar was to "prevent withdrawal" of disclosures "already in the possession of the public" by the issuance of a patent.

Thus, throughout our case law, public accessibility has been the criterion by which a prior art reference will be judged for the purposes of § 102(b). Oftentimes courts have found it helpful to rely on distribution and indexing as proxies for public accessibility. But when they have done so, it has not been to the exclusion of all other measures of public accessibility. In other words, distribution and indexing are not the only factors to be considered in a § 102(b) "printed publication" inquiry.

The determination of whether a reference is a "printed publication" under 35 U.S.C. § 102(b) involves a case-by-case inquiry into the facts and circumstances surrounding the reference's disclosure to members of the public. Accordingly, our analysis must begin with the facts of this case, none of which are in dispute.

In this case, the Liu reference was displayed to the public approximately two years before the '950 application filing date.

The reference was shown to a wide variety of viewers, a large subsection of whom possessed ordinary skill in the art of cereal chemistry and agriculture. Furthermore, the reference was prominently displayed for approximately three cumulative days at AACC and the AES at Kansas State University. The reference was shown with no stated expectation that the information would not be copied or reproduced by those viewing it. Finally, no copies of the Liu display were distributed to the public and the display was not later indexed in any database, catalog or library.

Given that the Liu reference was never distributed to the public and was never indexed, we must consider several factors relevant to the facts of this case before determining whether or not it was sufficiently publicly accessible in order to be considered a "printed publication" under § 102(b). These factors aid in resolving whether or not a temporarily displayed reference that was neither distributed nor indexed was nonetheless made sufficiently publicly accessible to count as a "printed publication" under § 102(b). The factors relevant to the facts of this case are: the length of time the display was exhibited, the expertise of the target audience, the existence (or lack thereof) of reasonable expectations that the material displayed would not be copied, and the simplicity or ease with which the material displayed could have been copied. Only after considering and balancing these factors can we determine whether or not the Liu reference was sufficiently publicly accessible to be a "printed publication" under § 102(b).

The duration of the display is important in determining the opportunity of the public in capturing, processing and retaining the information conveyed by the reference. The more transient the display, the less likely it is to be considered a "printed publication." Conversely, the longer a reference is displayed, the more likely it is to be considered a "printed publication." In this case, the Liu reference was displayed for a total of approximately three days. It was shown at the AACC meeting for approximately two and a half days and at the AES at Kansas State University for less than one day.

The expertise of the intended audience can help determine how easily those who viewed it could retain the displayed material. As Judge Learned Hand explained in *Jockmus v. Leviton*, 28 F.2d 812, 813-14 (2d Cir. 1928), a reference, "however ephemeral its existence," may be a "printed publication" if it "goes direct to those whose interests make them likely to observe and remember whatever it may contain that is new and useful." In this case, the intended target audience at the AACC meeting was comprised of cereal chemists and others having ordinary skill in the art of the '950 patent application. The intended viewers at the AES most likely also possessed ordinary skill in the art.

Whether a party has a reasonable expectation that the information it displays to the public will not be copied aids our § 102(b) inquiry. Where professional and behavioral norms entitle a party to a reasonable expectation that the information displayed will not be copied, we are more reluctant to find something a "printed publication." This reluctance helps preserve the incentive for inventors to participate in academic presentations or discussions. Where parties have taken steps to prevent the public from copying temporarily posted information, the opportunity for others to appropriate that information and assure its widespread public accessibility is reduced. These protective measures could include license agreements, non-disclosure agreements, anti-copying software or even a simple disclaimer informing members of the viewing public that no copying of the information will be allowed or countenanced. Protective measures are to be considered insofar as they create a reasonable expectation on the part of the inventor that the displayed information will not be copied. In this case, the appellants took no measures to protect the information they displayed—nor did the professional norms under which they were displaying their information entitle them to a reasonable expectation that their display would not be copied. There was no disclaimer discouraging copying, and any viewer was free to take notes from the Liu reference or even to photograph it outright.

Finally, the ease or simplicity with which a display could be copied gives further guidance to our § 102(b) inquiry. The more complex a display, the more difficult it will be for members of the public to effectively capture its information. The simpler a display is, the more likely members of the public could learn it by rote or take notes adequate enough for later reproduction. The Liu reference was made up of 14 separate slides. One slide was a title slide; one was an acknowledgement slide; and four others represented graphs and charts of experiment results. The other eight slides contained information presented in bullet point format, with no more than three bullet points to a slide. Further, no bullet point was longer than two concise sentences. Finally, as noted earlier, the fact that extrusion lowers cholesterol levels was already known by those who worked with SCF. The discovery disclosed in the Liu reference was that double extrusion increases this effect. As a result, most of the eight substantive slides only recited what had already been known in the field, and only a few slides presented would have needed to have been copied by an observer to capture the novel information presented by the slides.

Upon reviewing the above factors, it becomes clear that the Liu reference was sufficiently publicly accessible to count as a "printed publication" for the purposes of 35 U.S.C. § 102(b). The reference itself was shown for an extended period of time to members of the public having ordinary skill in the art of the invention behind the '950 patent application. Those members of the public were not precluded from taking notes or even photographs of the reference. And the reference itself was presented in such a way that copying of the information it contained would have been a relatively simple undertaking for those to whom it was exposed—particularly given the amount of time they had to copy the information and the lack of any restrictions on their copying of the information. For these reasons, we conclude that the Liu reference was made sufficiently publicly accessible to count as a "printed publication" under § 102(b).

What is the critical date of a printed publication?

According to *In re Schlittler* (C.C.P.A. 1956), "[T]he mere placing of a manuscript in the hands of a publisher does not necessarily make it available to the public within the meaning of [the printed publication limitation]." Similarly, according to *E. I. du Pont de Nemours & Co. v. Cetus Corp.* (N.D. Cal. 1990), sending a grant proposal to a limited number of expert reviewers is not a publication under 35 U.S.C. 102a. The critical date, therefore, is generally considered the date that the printed publication becomes available to the public.

What Is a Public Use?

In the late 1800s, an inventor constructed wooden pavements in the city of Elizabeth, New Jersey with his own money. The public used and the inventor examined these pavements nearly every day for 6 years before the inventor filed for a patent on the invention. In the *City of Elizabeth v. Pavement Company* case, the Supreme Court held that the experimental use of an invention by the inventor himself, despite being used by the public, is not a public use under 35 U.S.C. 102b. The Court stated that "If used under the surveillance of the inventor, and for the purpose of enabling him to test the machine... it will... be a mere experimental use, and not a public use."

A few years later, in 1881, the Supreme Court heard another public use case. In the *Egbert v. Lippmann* case, Barnes invented improved steels for a corset in early 1855. He presented these to his girlfriend, with neither an obligation of secrecy nor any other restriction. His girlfriend wore the steels for many years. Barnes filed a patent application in 1866. The Court held that an invention that is given to one person without any obligation of secrecy or any other restriction and is used even in a private manner can be a violation of the public use limitation under 35 U.S.C. 102b. In a rare moment of judicial humor, the Court declared, "The inventor slept on his rights for eleven years."

In recent cases, the Federal Circuit has focused on the nature and purpose of the use. Use for a commercial purpose is generally a public use, even if it is hidden from the public and even if it occurs only once. Use for personal interest or enjoyment, on the other hand, will generally not be considered a public use.

Non-Disclosure Agreements

A person shall not be entitled to a patent if the filing date of their patent application is filed more than 1 year after the occurrence of a printed publication of the invention in the United States or a foreign country, or a public use of the invention in the United States. What can be done to protect against this? An inventor can ask all of the recipients of a printed publication or the observers of the public use to sign a non-disclosure agreement (also known as an "NDA" or a confidentiality agreement), which will negate the "publicly accessible" aspect and will prevent the clock from ticking with regards to a printed publication and public use (but NOT to an on-sale event).

What Is an Offer for Sale?

According to the Supreme Court in *Pfaff v. Wells Electronics, Inc.* (1998), "[T]he on-sale bar applies when two conditions are satisfied before the critical date. First, the product must be the subject of a commercial offer for sale... Second, the invention must be ready for patenting [which] may be satisfied...by proof of reduction to practice before the critical date, or by proof that prior to the critical date the inventor had prepared [enabling] drawings or other descriptions of the invention...."

Foreign Filing Considerations

As discussed, the United States has a grace period that allows inventors to disclose their invention and then–within 1 year– file a patent application. No other country has a grace period like the United States.

In the rest of the world, an applicant is not entitled to a patent if their invention was publicly available before the filing date of their patent application. Information is considered to be "publicly available" when the public could possibly gain knowledge of the information without any restriction or obligation. This is known as the "absolute novelty" rule.

In the United States, an invention that is open to the public is considered to be in "public use" if it is possible to reverse engineer the invention. In Europe, however, an invention that is open to the public is considered to be "publicly available" if it does not require "great expense and difficultly" to reverse engineer the invention. Although these definitions are similar, the subtle difference often results in a loss of patent rights in one country, but not the other.

Avoiding the loss of patent rights in foreign countries...

What can be done to protect against this loss of patent rights in foreign countries? Again, the inventor can ask all of the receipts of a printed publication or the observers of the public use to sign a non-disclosure agreement (i.e., a confidentiality agreement). This will prevent the clock from ticking with regards to a printed publication and public use. The inventor may also prepare and file a provisional application, a "regular" patent application, or a "worldwide" patent application under the Rules of the Patent Cooperation Treaty (known as a "PCT" patent application). The strategies of filing patent applications will be discussed in later chapters.

How to Prepare and File a Provisional Application

Introduction

About one third of patent applications filed in the U.S. Patent Office are initially filed as a provisional application. As the name implies, a provisional application is a simpler and cheaper—albeit temporary—way to start the patent process. Filing a provisional application informs the patent office that the inventor possessed a particular invention on a particular date. As long as the inventor files a patent application (often clumsily called a "non-provisional application") within 1 year, the U.S.

Patent Office grants the patent application the "priority date" of the provisional application and evaluates the patent application as though it were filed on the filing date of the provisional application. Since more than 1,000 patent applications are filed on a daily basis, the grant of the earlier priority date might allow the patent application to be examined without literally thousands of intervening patent applications from other inventors.

Provisional applications do not require any claims. Since the claims are the most challenging aspect of a patent application, provisional applications can be prepared and filed faster and cheaper than a patent application. For this reason, provisional applications are often used when there is insufficient time to prepare a patent application and when costs prohibit the preparation of a patent application.

The filing of a provisional application can delay the filing of a patent application for 1 year, but it will not count toward the 20-year term of the patent. For this reason, provisional applications are also used when technology will likely undergo significant modifications in next 6 to 12 months and when invention will have high value at the end of the patent term.

Although a provisional patent is not a "real" patent application that will be examined, the filing of a provisional application permits use of the "Patent Pending" notice on the invention, which signals the serious intent of the inventor.

Five main elements are required for a provisional application, including:

1.   Written Description of the Invention
2.   Drawings of the Invention
3.   Filing Fee
4.   Cover Sheet or Application Data Sheet
5.   Submission of the Provisional Application

Written Description of the Invention

To gain the benefit of a provisional application, the provisional application must support the claims of a later filed patent application and adhere to the written description requirements (including the enablement rule and best mode rule) described above. The written description should include:

- Three or four essential elements (or "subsystems" or process steps)
- Function, manufacturing, and possible alternatives for each essential element
- Relationship of the essential elements to each other
- Additional elements that may be used with the invention
- Function, manufacturing, and possible alternatives for each additional element.

Practical advice

Amendments are not permitted in provisional applications; no new matter can be added to a filed provisional application. An inventor may, however, file an additional provisional application, which—if filed before the 1-year anniversary of the earliest

---

provisional application—can be combined with other provisional applications into a single patent application.

Using this strategy, an inventor can file a provisional application immediately upon conceiving a bright idea. If the idea becomes obsolete in a month (or if a superior idea trumps it), then the inventor can abandon the provisional application, losing only the filing fee and a little time. If the idea holds promise, then the inventor can subsequently prepare and file a patent application with the confidence that the application will receive the best possible filing date.

The U.S. Patent Office keeps all provisional applications secret unless they are the subject of a priority claim by a later patent application. Inventors, therefore, can change their minds later, possibly deciding to protect their inventions instead as trade secrets or, taking a completely different tack, sharing them as open-source projects. Since an abandoned provisional application is never published, it will never be considered a printed publication. Therefore, an inventor may file a provisional application, abandon the provisional application, and later file a regular application on the same invention (but without, of course, a priority claim to the abandoned provisional application).

Drawings

The provisional application must include drawing(s) "where necessary for the understanding of the subject matter sought to be patented." (See 35 U.S.C. §113.) The drawings for a device or system could include a top, front, bottom, elevation, perspective, partial, detailed, exploded, and/or cross-sectional view. The drawings for a process or method could include a flowchart, schematic representation.

Filing Fee

As of the writing of this text, the filing fee for a provisional application is $125 for a small entity and $250 for a large entity. (See 37 C.F.R. §1.16(d).) A small entity is any entity "whose number of employees, including affiliates, does not exceed 500 persons." (See 13 C.F.R. §121.802.)

Application Data Sheet

USPTO form SB/0016, which can be found at http://www.uspto.gov/forms/sb0016.pdf, should be used when submitting the provisional application. Although not required, this form helps the applicant identify the application as a provisional application, include the names and residences of the inventors, and include the title of the invention.

Who should be listed as an inventor?

Inventorship, as described above, is whether a person has made an original contribution to the conception of at least one of the *claims* in the patent application. Since provisional applications do not require (and often do not include) claims, who should be listed as an inventor? To gain the benefit of the earlier filing date of a provisional application, there must be at least one common inventor between the later patent application and the earlier

---

provisional application. Thus, it is advised that the provisional application names the inventors who would most likely be named in a later patent application.

Submission of the Provisional Application

An inventor may choose to either mail a hardcopy version of the provisional application or upload an electronic version of the provisional application. When mailing a patent application with the USPTO, the applicant should use the Express Mailing option at the United States Postal Service. "Any correspondence received by the USPTO that was delivered by the "Express Mail Post Office to Addressee" service of the United States Postal Service will be considered filed with the USPTO on the date of deposit with the USPS." (See 37 C.F.R. §1.10.) Correspondence not delivered by the Express Mail option (even mail delivered by other overnight services such as Federal Express) will *not* be considered filed with the USPTO on the date that it was *filed*. Instead, it will be considered filed on the date that it was *received*.

The next steps...

To avoid abandonment of a provisional application, the inventor must file a regular patent application within 1 year of the filing of the provisional application. Some inventors are tempted to simply buy a book and try to go it alone because the cost of preparing and filing a regular patent application is so high. Be forewarned, however: The main difference between a provisional and a regular patent application is the inclusion of claims in a regular patent application, which define the legal protection afforded to the invention.

Writing claims, as once declared by the U.S. Supreme Court, is one of the trickiest challenges in the legal world. The inclusion of an extra word or phrase in a claim can make the difference between a broad and valuable patent versus a narrow and worthless patent. To avoid banking your business on a legal pitfall, inventors, the United States Patent and Trademark Office, and–of course–patent attorneys and agents recommend that inventors find a registered patent attorney or agent for preparing and filing a patent application.

Chapter Six

Does the Invention Infringe Any Patents?

Chapter Contents

- Introduction
    - Infringement Lawsuit
    - Focus on the Claims
- Infringement Analysis
    - Introduction
    - Interpretation of the Claims
    - Literal Infringement
- Infringement under the Doctrine of Equivalents
    - Introduction
    - Case Law
    - Limitations on the Reach of the Doctrine of Equivalents
- Infringement Through Other Actions
    - Active Inducement
    - Contributory Infringement
- Defenses
    - Introduction
    - Statute
    - Laches and Equitable Estoppel
- Remedies
    - Introduction
    - Injunctions
    - Damages
    - Triple Damages under Willful Infringement
    - Options of the Accused Infringer
- How to Design Around Problematic Patents

Introduction

Under the patent statutes, patent infringement occurs when a party—without permission of the patent owner—makes, uses, offers to sell, or sells the invention covered by the patent during the term of the patent. 35 U.S.C. § 271a. The patentee (i.e., the entity that owns that patent that is being infringed) has the right to enforce their patent rights and therefore has the right to prevent others from making, using, and/or selling their invention. The patentee may enforce the rights of their patent by initiating an infringement lawsuit.

Use of the word "Infringing"

During a patentability analysis, a claim may *read on* the disclosure of a patent (in a §102 novelty rejection), or may *read on* a combination of the disclosures from several patents (in a §103 obviousness rejection). A claim of a patent cannot, however, *infringe* a patent—only the acts of making, using, offering to sell, selling, and importing can infringe another patent.

Infringement Lawsuit

If a patent is infringed, the patentee may initiate a lawsuit in federal court. The lawsuit may include a request to force the infringer to stop making, using, and selling the patented invention (an "injunction"), and may include a request to force the infringer to pay for past infringements ("damages"). Upon the initiation of an infringement lawsuit, the accused infringer may argue that their actions do not actually infringe the patent;

the accused infringer may also argue that the allegedly infringed patent is invalid.

According to an article for the *Quarterly Journal of the American Intellectual Property Law Association*, based on recent data, patentees win only 25% of infringement lawsuits. Not surprisingly, the financial strength of the patentee is a strong factor correlating to the outcome of infringement lawsuits. For example, individual patentees have only half as good a chance as corporations to win patent infringement lawsuits. Similarly, the authors of the article concluded that it is fairly difficult for patent owners, of whatever income level, to win a patent infringement lawsuit against an accused infringer that has revenues in excess of $1 billion.

If either the plaintiff or the defense is displeased with the holding of the infringement lawsuit, the case may be appealed. From the district court, one can appeal to the Court of Appeals for the Federal Circuit (CAFC), which hears all patent appeals. From the CAFC, one can appeal to the Supreme Court of the United States.

Who is infringing my patent?

For a patent owner to enforce their patent rights, they must know against whom to enforce their rights (i.e., who is potentially infringing their patent). One method of determining these potential infringes is by noting the issued patents that cite your patent in the "References Cited" section. If an issued patent covers an improvement over your patented invention and they are making, using, or selling their improvement, they may be potentially infringing your patent. If they are not making, using, or selling their invention, they may be interested in licensing your patent to do so.

Focus on the Claims

The coverage of the patent is defined by the claims. *Corning Glass Works v. Sumitomo USA* (Fed. Cir. 1989). A patent owner need only prove infringement of a single claim to establish patent infringement. *Intervet America, Inc. v. Kee-Vet Lab, Inc.* (Fed. Cir. 1989). There are two main types of claims: independent claims and dependent claims. A dependent claim includes all of the limitations of the claims on which it depends, plus additional limitations. Thus, if the independent claim is not infringed, the dependent claims cannot be infringed. *Wolverine World Wide, Inc. v. Nike, Inc.* (Fed. Cir. 1994) (quoting *Wahpeton Canvas Co. v. Frontier, Inc.*, 870 F.2d 1546, 1553, (Fed. Cir. 1989). For this reason, to determine infringement of a claim or claims, the analysis will focus on the *independent claims* (as apposed to the *dependent claims*) of a patent.

Independent and dependent claims

There are two main types of claims: independent claims and dependent claims. An independent claim includes any number of elements and may include various features or characteristics of those elements. These elements and features are known as claim limitations.

A dependent claim depends on a previously listed claim (independent or dependent). The dependent claim includes all of the limitations of the claims on which the dependent claim depends *plus* additional limitations. In order to infringe a claim, the accused device or method must include *every* limitation recited in the claim. Therefore, if an independent claim of a patent is not infringed, the dependent claims that depend from that independent claim cannot be infringed. For this reason, an infringement analysis focuses on the independent claims of a patent.

Infringement Analysis

Introduction

If a patent infringement lawsuit is initiated, an infringement analysis is typically conducted at least three times: first by the patentee to determine if a person or entity is infringing their patent, second by the accused infringer to determine if their actions actually infringe the patent, and third by the court to determine if the alleged infringer actually infringes the patent. The determination of whether an accused product or method infringes a claim of a patent includes two steps: (1) interpreting the claim and (2) comparing the interpreted claim with the accused product or method. *Markman v. Westview Instr., Inc.* (Fed. Cir. 1995). There are two versions of the comparison step: literal infringement and infringement under the doctrine of equivalents.

Interpretation of the Claims

A typical claim includes several elements or limitations. The presence of a particularly novel or unobvious element or limitation does not make the other elements or limitations insignificant. According to *Lantech, Inc. v. Keip Mach Co.*, all of the limitations of a claim are meaningful. The words and phrases of a claim are given their ordinary and accustomed meaning, except in the following situations:

(1) When "a patent applicant has elected to be a lexicographer by providing an explicit definition in the specification for a claim term...the definition selected by the patent applicant controls...." See *Renishaw PLC v. Marposs Societa' Per Azioni* (Fed. Cir. 1998). The patent rules allow an application to define their own vocabulary (e.g., to be their own lexicographer) because it is often difficult—especially with pioneering inventions—to describe a "new" invention with "old" words and phrases. By its definition, a patentable invention has never been described or taught before. Thus, as the CAFC declared in the *Renishaw PLC v. Marposs Societa' Per Azioni* case, "[t]he law provides a patentee with this opportunity because... there may not be an extant term of singular meaning for the structure or concept that is being claimed."

(2) "[W]here the term or terms chosen by the patentee so deprive the claim of clarity that there is no means by which the scope of the claim may be ascertained[, then the] term or terms used in the claim invites—or indeed, requires—reference to intrinsic, or in some cases, extrinsic, evidences...." See *Johnson Worldwide Associates, Inc. v.*

Zebco Corp. (Fed. Cir. 1999). Two types of evidence can be introduced to aid the interpretation of the claims: intrinsic (or internal) and extrinsic (or external). Intrinsic evidence includes other claims of the patent (through claim differentiation); the specification of the patent; and the prosecution history of the patent. Extrinsic evidence includes expert testimony; inventor testimony; dictionaries, technical treatises, and articles. According to the CAFC in *Vitronics Corp. v. Conceptronic, Inc.*, "In most situations, an analysis of the intrinsic evidence alone will resolve any ambiguity in a disputed claim term. In such circumstances, it is improper to rely on extrinsic evidence."

(3) When the patent applicant has made statements during the prosecution of the patent, these statements will limit the meaning of the element of the claim. See *Spectrum Intl., Inc. v. Sterilite Corp.* (Fed. Cir. 1998). Statements made during the prosecution of a patent are kept with the prosecution file history. The USPTO makes files histories available for published patents on the "public PAIR" portal. (http://portal.uspto.gov/external/portal/pair) Statements made by the applicant are typically found in documents entitled "Response After Non-Final Action."

Literal Infringement

Once the claims have been properly interpreted, the next step is to compare the interpreted claim with the accused product or method. There are two versions of the comparison step: literal infringement and infringement under the doctrine of equivalents (described in the next section). Literal infringement of a claim exists when every element or limitation recited in the claim is found in the accused device or method. In most cases, it does not matter that the accused device or method includes additional elements.

Very few court cases address the issue of literal infringement. Literal infringement is not rare, but so little disputes have been appealed to higher courts regarding literal infringement. Most parties simply settle infringement lawsuits that involve literal infringement. Far more common is the issue of infringement under the doctrine of equivalents.

Comprehension question on literal infringement

U.S. Patent No. 6,584,450 assigned to Netflix.com, Inc. and entitled "Method and Apparatus for Renting Items" includes the following claim:

31.   A method for renting movies to customers, the method comprising the computer-implemented steps of:

a)   receiving one or more movie selection criteria from a customer that indicates one or more movies that the customer desires to rent;

b)   providing to the customer up to a specified number of the one or more movies indicated by the one or more movie selection criteria; and

c)   in response to a return of any of the movies provided to the customer, providing to the customer one or more other movies indicated by the one or more movie selection criteria, wherein a total current number of movies provided to the customer does not exceed the specified number.

Suppose you implement an online service that (a) received a list of the following movies: "Brazil," "The Fisher King," and "Twelve Monkeys" from a user; (b) sent "Brazil" and "The Fisher King" to the user; and (c) after the user returns "Brazil," you sent "Twelve Monkeys" to the user? This would appear to infringe Claim 31, and thus infringe U.S. Patent No. 6,584,450.

As a side note, Netflix sued Blockbuster for patent infringement of U.S. Patent No. 6,584,450. The lawsuit was settled in 2007.

Infringement Under the Doctrine of Equivalents

Introduction

The doctrine of equivalents attempts to strike a balance between ensuring that the patentee enjoys the full benefit of his or her patent and ensuring that the claims give "fair notice" of the patent's scope. Infringement under the doctrine of equivalents exists when literal infringement does not exist, but the differences between the accused product or method and the claimed invention are *insubstantial*.

Case Law

The following section includes an excerpt from the 1950 Supreme Court case *Graver Tank & Mfg. Co. v. Linde Air* that describes the test used to determine infringement under the doctrine of equivalents.

Graver Tank & Mfg. Co. v. Linde Air (1950)

MR. JUSTICE JACKSON delivered the opinion of the Court.

Linde Air Products Co., owner of the Jones patent for an electric welding process and for fluxes to be used with the electric welding process, brought an action for infringement against Lincoln and the two Graver companies. The trial court held four flux claims valid and infringed and certain other flux claims and all process claims invalid. The Court of Appeals affirmed findings of validity and infringement as to the four flux claims but reversed the trial court and held valid the process claims and the remaining contested flux claims.

At the outset it should be noted that the single issue before us is whether the trial court's holding that the four flux claims have been infringed will be sustained.

In determining whether an accused device or composition infringes a valid patent, resort must be had in the first instance to the words of the claim. If accused matter falls clearly within the claim, infringement is made out and that is the end of it. But courts have also recognized that to permit imitation of a patented invention which does not copy every literal detail would be to convert the protection of the patent grant into a hollow and useless thing. Such a limitation would leave room for—indeed encourage—the unscrupulous copyist to make unimportant and insubstantial changes and substitutions in the patent which, though adding nothing, would be enough to take the copied matter outside the claim, and hence outside the reach of law....

The doctrine of equivalents evolved in response to this experience. The essence of the doctrine is that one may not practice a fraud on a patent. Originating almost a century ago in the case of *Winans v. Denmead*, it has been consistently applied by this Court and the lower federal courts, and continues today ready and available for utilization when the proper circumstances for its application arise. "To temper unsparing logic and prevent an infringer from stealing the benefit of an invention" a patentee may invoke this doctrine to proceed against the producer of a device "if it performs substantially the same function in substantially the same way to obtain the same result." See *Sanitary Refrigerator Co. v. Winters*. The theory on which it is founded is that "if two devices do the same work in substantially the same way, and accomplish substantially the same result, they are the same, even though they differ in name, form, or shape." See *Machine Co. v. Murphy*. The doctrine operates not only in favor of the patentee of a pioneer or primary invention, but also for the patentee of a secondary invention consisting of a combination of old ingredients which produce new and useful results, although the area of equivalence may vary under the circumstances.
...

What constitutes equivalency must be determined against the context of the patent, the prior art, and the particular circumstances of the case. Equivalence, in the patent law, is not the prisoner of a formula and is not an absolute to be considered in a vacuum. It does not require complete identity for every purpose and in every respect. In determining equivalents, things equal to the same thing may not be equal to each other and, by the same token, things for most purposes different may sometimes be equivalents. Consideration must be given to the purpose for which an ingredient is used in a patent, the qualities it has when combined with the other ingredients, and the function which it is intended to perform. An important factor is whether persons reasonably skilled in the art would have known of the interchangeability of an ingredient not contained in the patent with one that was.

...

In the case before us, we have two electric welding compositions or fluxes: the patented composition, Unionmelt Grade 20, and the accused composition, Lincolnweld 660. The patent under which Unionmelt is made claims essentially a combination of alkaline earth metal silicate and calcium fluoride; Unionmelt actually contains, however, silicates of calcium and magnesium, two alkaline earth metal silicates. Lincolnweld's composition is similar to Unionmelt's, except that it substitutes silicates of calcium and manganese - the latter not an alkaline earth metal - for silicates of calcium and magnesium. In all other respects, the two compositions are alike. The mechanical methods in which these compositions are employed are similar. They are identical in operation and produce the same kind and quality of weld.

The question which thus emerges is whether the substitution of the manganese which is not an alkaline earth metal for the magnesium which is, under the circumstances of this case, and in view of the technology and the prior art, is a change of such substance as to make the doctrine of equivalents inapplicable; or conversely, whether under the circumstances the change was so insubstantial that the trial court's invocation of the doctrine of equivalents was justified.

Without attempting to be all-inclusive, we note the following evidence in the record: Chemists familiar with the two fluxes testified that manganese and magnesium were similar in many of their reactions. There is testimony by a metallurgist that alkaline earth metals are often found in manganese ores in their natural state and that they serve the same purpose in the fluxes; and a chemist testified that "in the sense of the patent" manganese could be included as an alkaline earth metal. Much of this testimony was corroborated by reference to recognized texts on inorganic chemistry. Particularly important, in addition, were the disclosures of the prior art, also contained in the record. The Miller patent, No. 1,754,566, which preceded the patent in suit, taught the use of manganese silicate in welding fluxes. Manganese was similarly disclosed in the Armor patent, No. 1,467,825, which also described a welding composition. And the record contains no evidence of any kind to show that Lincolnweld was developed as the result of independent research or experiments.

...

The trial judge found on the evidence before him that the Lincolnweld flux and the composition of the patent in suit are substantially identical in operation and in result. He found also that Lincolnweld is in all respects equivalent to Unionmelt for welding purposes. And he concluded that "for all practical purposes, manganese silicate can be efficiently and effectually substituted for calcium and magnesium silicates as the major constituent of the welding composition." These conclusions are adequately supported by the record; certainly they are not clearly erroneous.

It is difficult to conceive of a case more appropriate for application of the doctrine of equivalents. The disclosures of the prior art made clear that manganese silicate was a useful ingredient in welding compositions. Specialists familiar with the problems of welding compositions understood that manganese was equivalent to and could be substituted for magnesium in the composition of the patented flux and their observations were confirmed by the literature of chemistry. Without some explanation or indication that Lincolnweld was developed by independent research, the trial court could properly infer that the accused flux is the result of imitation rather than experimentation or invention. Though infringement was not literal, the changes which avoid literal infringement are colorable only. We conclude that the trial court's judgment of infringement respecting the four flux claims was proper, and we adhere to our prior decision on this aspect of the case.

Affirmed.

Limitations on the Reach of the Doctrine of Equivalents
The reach of the doctrine of equivalents is limited by (1) the scope of the prior art—the doctrine of equivalents cannot be used

to extend the scope of the patent claims to cover an accused product or method found in the prior art or obvious in view of the prior art. *See Key Mfg. Group v. Microdot, Inc.* (Fed. Cir. 1991); (2) the "all elements rule"—the doctrine of equivalents cannot be used if even one element of a claim or its equivalent is not present in the accused product. *Pennwalt. v. Durand-Wayland, Inc.* (Fed. Cir. 1987); and (3) the prosecution history estoppel rule, which is described below.

As held by the Federal Circuit in *Festo Corp. v. Shoketsu Kinzoku Kogyo Kabushiki Co., Ltd.* (Fed. Cir. 2003), prosecution history estoppel prevents the patent owner from recapturing subject matter that was disclaimed or relinquished with an amendment of the claim during the prosecution of the patent. Prosecution history estoppel applies to amendments that (1) narrow or limit the literal scope of a claim and (2) are made for a reason that is substantially related to the patentability of the claim.

A narrowing amendment found to have been made for a 'substantial reason related to patentability' is then subject to the *Festo* presumption, which was established by the Supreme Court in *Festo Corp. v. Shoketsu Kinzoku Kogyo Kabushiki Co., Ltd.* (2002). The *Festo* presumption states that the "patentee has surrendered all territory between the original claim limitation and the amended claim limitation." The *Festo* presumption may be overcome by demonstrating one of the following: (1) "that the alleged equivalent would have been unforeseeable at the time of the narrowing amendment, (2) that the rationale underlying the narrowing amendment bore no more than a tangential relation to the equivalent in question, or (3) that there was 'some other reason' suggesting that the patentee could not reasonably have been expected to have described the equivalent." As stated by the Supreme Court, "If the patentee fails to rebut the Festo presumption, then prosecution history estoppel bars the patentee from relying on the doctrine of equivalents for the accused element."

Notes

In rejecting the American-style Doctrine of Equivalents, the Lord Hoffman (of the British High Court) noted: "I cannot say that I am sorry [that our precedent is antithetical to the doctrine of equivalents] because the *Festo* litigation suggests, with all respect to the courts of the United States, that American patent litigants pay dearly for results which are no more just or predictable than could be achieved by simply reading the claims." See *Kirin-Amgen Inc and Others v. Hoechst Marion Roussel Limited and Others* [2004] UKHL 46.

Lord Hoffman is referring to the rule, the exception, the exception to the exception, and the exception to the exception to the exception, as follows:

1) Rule (Literal Infringement): every limitation is found in the accused device.
2) Exception (Doctrine of Equivalents): when the differences between the accused device and the claimed invention are insubstantial.

3) Exception to the Exception (Prosecution History Estoppel): when the subject matter that was disclaimed or relinquished during the prosecution.

4) Exception to the Exception to the Exception (Festo Exception): when (1) "that the alleged equivalent would have been unforeseeable at the time of the narrowing amendment, (2) that the rationale underlying the narrowing amendment bore no more than a tangential relation to the equivalent in question, or (3) that there was 'some other reason' suggesting that the patentee could not reasonably have been expected to have described the equivalent."

Infringement Through Other Actions

Contributory Infringement

Though not a direct infringer, a party can be held liable for contributory infringement of a patent. Under the patent statutes, contributory infringement occurs when a party—without permission of the patent owner—offers to sell or sells a component of a patented invention such that a later user directly infringes the patent. 35 U.S.C. § 271(c). When asserting contributory infringement, a patent owner must prove that the alleged contributory infringer knew that the combination for which its components was especially made was both patented and infringing. *Preemption Devices v. Minnesota Mining & Mfg.* (Fed. Cir. 1986). Furthermore, the patent owner must prove that the component is not a "staple article" suitable for substantial noninfringing use.

Active Inducement

A party who does not directly or contributorily infringe a patent can also be liable under a theory of active inducement. 35 U.S.C. § 271(b). To prove active inducement, a patent owner must prove that the seller had the *specific intent* to encourage another to infringe the patent. *Manville Sales Corp. v. Paramount Sys., Inc.* (Fed. Cir. 1990). In contrast to contributory infringement, mere knowledge of the acts alleged to constitute direct infringement is insufficient proof. The concept of active inducement exists to protect patent rights from subversion by those who, without directly infringing the patent themselves, engage in acts designed to facilitate infringement by others. *Oak Indus. Inc. v. Zenith Elecs. Corp.* (N.D. IL 1989). Active steps that can be found to be inducement of infringement include advertising, labeling, and providing instructions that cause or encourage another to infringe a patent with knowledge of the likely infringing result.

Defenses

Introduction

A defense to an accusation of infringement is not a denial of the infringement, but rather an attack on the ability of the patent to meet the requirements of the patent laws or an attack on the behavior of the applicant (known as "inequitable conduct") to remove or limit the rights of the patentee to enforce their patent. A defense may also be an excuse or justification of the infringement (e.g., "laches").

Statute

"A patent shall be presumed valid. Each claim of a patent (whether in independent, dependent, or multiple dependent form) shall be presumed valid independently of the validity of other claims; dependent ... claims shall be presumed valid even though dependent upon an invalid claim.... The burden of establishing invalidity of a patent or any claim thereof shall rest on the party asserting such invalidity.

The following shall be defenses in any action involving the... infringement of a patent...

- Invalidity of ... any claim in suit on any ground specified... as a condition for patentability [including the utility, novelty, and unobviousness requirements],
- Invalidity of ... any claim in suit for failure to comply with any requirement of sections 112 [including the written description and enablement requirements] or 251...."

(35 U.S.C. 282)

Laches and Equitable Estoppel

The person invoking laches asserts that an opposing party has "slept on its rights" and that, as a result of this delay, the opposing party is no longer entitled to its original claim. Two elements underlie the defense of laches: (a) the patentee's delay in bringing suit was unreasonable and inexcusable; and (b) the alleged infringer suffered material prejudice attributable to the delay. A *presumption* of laches arises when a patentee delays bringing suit for more than 6 years after the date the patentee knew or should have known of the alleged infringer's activity.

Three elements must be established to bar a patentee's suit by reason of equitable estoppel: (a) the patentee, through misleading conduct (which may include specific statements, action, inaction, or silence where there was an obligation to speak), led the alleged infringer to reasonably infer that the patentee does not intend to enforce its patent against the alleged infringer, (b) the alleged infringer relies on that conduct, and (c) due to its reliance, the alleged infringer will be materially prejudiced if the patentee is allowed to proceed with its claim. No presumption is applicable to the defense of equitable estoppel. In the most common situation, an immediate or vigorous threat of enforcement, followed by silence for an unreasonably long time, will result in equitable estoppel. See *ABB Robotics, Inc. v. GMFanuc Robotics Corp.* (Fed. Cir. 1995).

Remedies

Introduction

There are two major types of remedies in patent law: injunctions and damages. An injunction is typically granted for an anticipated infringement; damages are typically granted for past infringement. In certain cases, the damage award can be tripled to punish the infringer for particular actions.

Injunctions

The "courts... may grant injunctions in accordance with the principles of equity to prevent the violation of any right secured by patent, on such terms as the court deems reasonable." (35 U.S.C. 283).

An injunction is a court order preventing a particular party from taking a particular action or stopping a particular party from continuing to take a particular action. In patent law, an injunction is a court order preventing an infringer from making, using, or selling the claimed subject matter of a particular patent. Injunctions come in two flavors: preliminary and permanent. Preliminary injunctions are often issued to allow fact-finding so a judge can determine whether a permanent injunction is justified.

According to CAFC in the *H.H. Robertson Co. v. United Steel Deck, Inc.* case, "An applicant for a preliminary injunction against patent infringement must show... (1) a reasonable probability of eventual success in the litigation and (2) that the movant will be irreparably injured... if relief is not granted.... [T]he district court should [also] take into account... (3) the possibility of harm to other interested persons..., and (4) the public interest."

Although a departure from other areas of the law, the general rule of permanent injunctions in patent law was that a "permanent injunction will issue once infringement and validity have been adjudged." The Supreme Court case of *eBay v. MercExchange* (2006), however, changed this general rule and replaced it with the four-part test used for preliminary permanent injunctions (and used in other areas of the law). In that case, MercExchange sought to license its business method patent to eBay, but no agreement was reached. In the subsequent patent infringement suit, a jury found that the MercExchange patent was valid, that eBay had infringed the patent, and that damages were appropriate. Instead of shutting down eBay, as was expected, the Supreme Court applied the traditional four-factor test.

Damages

"Upon finding for the [patent owner,] the court shall award the [patent owner] damages adequate to compensate for the infringement, but in no event less than a reasonable royalty for the use made of the invention by the infringer...." (35 U.S.C. 284).

According to the Sixth Circuit in *Panduit Corp. v. Stahlin Bros. Fibre Works, Inc.*, to obtain lost profits "a patent owner must prove: (1) demand for the patented product, (2) absence of acceptable noninfringing substitutes, (3) his manufacturing and marketing capability to exploit the demand, and (4) the amount of the profit he would have made." The court further stated that: "When actual damages, e.g., lost profits cannot be proved, the patent owner is entitled to a reasonable royalty. A reasonable royalty is an amount which a person, desiring to manufacture and sell a patented article, as a business proposition, would be willing to pay as a royalty and yet be able to make and sell the patented article, in the market, at a reasonable profit."

A patentee who makes or sells a patented product, or a person who does so for the patentee, is required to mark the product with the word "Patent" and the number of the patent. If the product is not properly marked, the patentee may not recover damages from an infringer unless the infringer was properly notified of the infringement and continued to infringe after the notice.

It is illegal to mark an article as patented when it is not in fact patented; the offender is subject to a penalty. One can mark articles sold with the terms "Patent Applied For" or "Patent Pending." These phrases have no legal effect; they simply provide notice that an application for patent has been filed in the Patent and Trademark Office. The protection afforded by a patent does not start until the actual grant of the patent.

Large damage awards

Damage awards can be immense. In 1990, the courts awarded Polariod $800M based on an infringement of their patents by Kodak. And, in 2012, the courts awarded Apple $1B based on an infringement of their patents by Samsung.

Triple Damages Under Willful Infringement

"The court may increase the damages up to three times the amount found or assessed." (35 U.S.C. 284)

According to the CAFC in *Underwater Devices, Inc. v. Morrison-Knudsen Co., Inc.*, a person with actual notice of another's patent rights has an affirmative duty to exercise due care to determine whether his or her acts will be infringing. This duty includes the duty to seek and follow competent legal advice before beginning activities that may constitute patent infringement. According to a study by Prof. Kimberly A. Moore of George Mason School of Law, willfulness is pleaded 92.7% of time.

Avoiding Triple Damages

To avoid an infringement lawsuit for a new product (and possibility of triple damages for willful infringement), a party should:

- Perform a Clearance Search after the design, but before the production
- In some situations, perform a State-of-the-Art Search for an entire product line to understand the "patent landscape", and
- Obtain a Clearance Opinion on the potentially problematic patents from a registered patent attorney.

Options of the Accused Infringer

The accused infringer in a patent infringement lawsuit typically has three options: (1) prove that the product omits an element of the claims; (2) invalidate the patent by proving the invention was either not novel or was obvious in light of the prior art; or (3) obtain permission from the patent owner through a license and royalty agreement. The accused infringer may be able to limit the damages and remedies owed to the patent holder if the accuser ceases the manufacturing and selling of the product, or modifies the product to omit an element of the claims, which is also called "designing around the patent."

Playing Hardball

If these three options have been exhausted, the accused infringer may also consider buying an issued patent that the patent owner, in their manufacturing or sale of their own products, infringes. This can often lead to a cross-licensing arrangement instead of a full-blown patent infringement lawsuit.

How to Design Around a Problematic Patent

When an infringement analysis has been conducted and the results are unfavorable, the process of designing around the problematic patent may result in the avoidance of an infringement. Although the process of designing around a problematic patent is far easier to explain than to execute, the process generally includes the following four steps:

(1) Interpret each of the elements of the independent claims using the above teachings and focusing on the independent claims. Mark the elements that were amended during prosecution because these elements might not be given the benefit of the doctrine of equivalents.

(2) Identify the elements of the claims that absolutely must be included in your product or service by paying careful attention to every word. If there are no remaining elements, return to step (1) and try again.

(3) From the remaining elements, identify an element that is common between the independent claims. If this is not possible, identify as few elements as possible amongst the various independent claims. Give precedent to the marked elements that were amended during prosecution.

(4) Modify your product or process so that your product or process completely omits the element. If the element was not amended during prosecution, ensure that your product or process does not perform substantially the same function in substantially the same way to obtain the same result as the element.

Chapter Seven

Who Owns the Patent Application?

Chapter Contents

- Who Is an Inventor?
    - Introduction
    - Case Law
- Who Is the Owner?
    - Introduction
    - Case Law
- Comparison of Assignments and Licenses
    - Introduction to Assignments
    - Introduction to Licenses
    - Inclusion of "Know How"

Who Is an Inventor?

Introduction

An error in inventorship (e.g., listing the wrong inventors or listing too few or too many inventors) that occurs without deceptive intent can be corrected. However, an error in inventorship that occurs with deceptive intent can lead to the invalidation of the entire patent. For this reason, understanding who should be named as an inventor is an important aspect of the patent application process. The following section includes a court decision on inventorship issues.

According to the patent laws, a person is not entitled to a patent if he did not himself invent the subject matter sought to be patented. See 35 U.S.C. §102. The inventor of patent application is the individual (not a corporation) who conceived of the invention in the claims. Conception has been characterized as "the complete performance of the mental part of the inventive act" and it is "the formation in the mind of the inventor of a definite and permanent idea of the complete and operative invention as it is thereafter to be applied in practice...." See *Townsend v. Smith* (CCPA 1930).

As technologies become more advanced, it often takes a team of inventors to conceive of the "complete and operative invention." Commonly more than one individual who has conceived of the invention to be patented; each of these individuals should be listed as an inventor. Multiple inventors on a patent application are known as *joint inventors*. "Inventors may apply for a patent jointly even though (1) they did not physically work together or at the same time, (2) each did not make the same type or amount of contribution, or (3) each did not make a contribution to the subject matter of every claim of the patent." 35 U.S.C. 116. Therefore, each inventor listed may have worked at different times in different locations; they may make contributions to the invention that differ in scope or investment of time and resources. They also may contribute to only one or more claims in the application.

Case Law

This section includes an excerpt from the 1998 Federal Circuit case of *Ethicon Inc. v. U.S. Surgical Corp.* that explains and applies the inventorship test.

Ethicon Inc. v. U.S. Surgical Corp. (Fed. Cir. 1998)

Circuit Judge Rader for the court:

I. BACKGROUND

U.S. Patent No. 4,535,773 (the '773 patent) relates to trocars, an essential tool for endoscopic surgery. A trocar is a surgical instrument which makes small incisions in the wall of a body cavity, often the abdomen, to admit endoscopic instruments. Trocars include a shaft within an outer sleeve. One end of the shaft has a sharp blade. At the outset of surgery, the surgeon uses the blade to puncture the wall and extend the trocar into the cavity. The surgeon then removes the shaft, leaving the hollow outer sleeve, through which the surgeon may insert tiny cameras and surgical instruments for the operation.

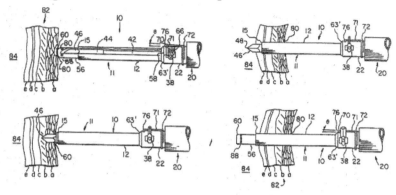

Conventional trocars, however, pose a risk of damage to internal organs or structures. As the trocar blade punctures the cavity wall, the sudden loss of resistance can cause the blade to lunge forward and injure an internal organ. The '773 patent claims a trocar that alleviates this danger. In one embodiment, the invention equips the trocar with a blunt, spring-loaded rod. As the trocar pierces the cavity wall, the rod automatically springs forward to precede the blade and shield against injury. A second embodiment has a retractable trocar blade that springs back into a protective sheath when it passes through the cavity wall. The patent also teaches the use of an electronic sensor in the end of the blade to signal the surgeon at the moment of puncture.

Yoon is a medical doctor and inventor of numerous patented devices for endoscopic surgery. In the late 1970s, Yoon began to conceive of a safety device to prevent accidental injury during trocar incisions. Yoon also conceived of a device to alert the surgeon when the incision was complete. In 1980, Yoon met Choi, an electronics technician, who had some college training in physics, chemistry, and electrical engineering, but no college degree. Choi had worked in the research and development of electronic devices. After Choi had demonstrated to Yoon some of the devices he had developed, Yoon asked Choi to work with him on several projects, including one for safety trocars. Choi was not paid for his work.

In 1982, after collaborating for approximately eighteen months, their relationship ended. Choi believed that Yoon found his work unsatisfactory and unlikely to produce any marketable product. For these reasons, Choi withdrew from cooperation with Yoon. In the same year, however, Yoon filed an application for a patent disclosing various embodiments of a safety trocar. Without informing Choi, Yoon named himself as the sole inventor. In 1985, the Patent and Trademark Office issued the '773 patent to Yoon, with fifty-five claims. Yoon thereafter granted an exclusive license under this patent to Ethicon. Yoon did not inform Choi of the patent application or issuance.

In 1989, Ethicon filed suit against U.S. Surgical for infringement of claims 34 and 50 of the '773 patent. In 1992, while this suit was still pending, U.S. Surgical became aware of Choi, and contacted him regarding his involvement in Yoon's safety trocar project. When Choi confirmed his role in the safety trocar project, U.S. Surgical obtained from Choi a "retroactive license" to practice "Choi's trocar related inventions." Under the license, Choi agreed to assist U.S. Surgical in any suit regarding the '773 patent. For its part, U.S. Surgical agreed to pay Choi contingent on its ultimate ability to continue to practice and market the invention. With the license in hand, U.S. Surgical moved to correct inventorship of the '773 patent under 35 U.S.C. § 256, claiming that Choi was a co-inventor of claims 23, 33, 46, and 47. Following an extensive hearing, the district court granted U.S. Surgical's motion, finding that Choi had contributed to the subject matter of claims 33 and 47.

U.S. Surgical next moved for dismissal of the infringement suit, arguing that Choi, as a joint owner of the patent, had granted it a valid license under the patent. By its terms, the license purported to grant rights to use the patent extending retroactively back to its issuance. The district court granted U.S. Surgical's motion and dismissed the suit.

...

II. CO-INVENTORSHIP

...

A patented invention may be the work of two or more joint inventors. See 35 U.S.C. § 116 (1994). Because "[c]onception is the touchstone of inventorship," each joint inventor must generally contribute to the conception of the invention. "Conception is the 'formation in the mind of the inventor, of a definite and permanent idea of the complete and operative invention, as it is hereafter to be applied in practice.'" An idea is sufficiently "definite and permanent" when "only ordinary skill would be necessary to reduce the invention to practice, without extensive research or experimentation."

The conceived invention must include every feature of the subject matter claimed in the patent. Nevertheless, for the conception of a joint invention, each of the joint inventors need not "make the same type or amount of contribution" to the invention. 35 U.S.C. § 116. Rather, each needs to perform only a part of the task which produces the invention. On the other hand, one does not qualify as a joint inventor by merely assisting the actual inventor after conception of the claimed invention. One who simply provides the inventor with well-known principles or explains the state of the art without ever having "a firm and definite idea" of the claimed combination as a whole does not qualify as a joint inventor. Moreover, depending on the scope of a patent's claims, one of ordinary skill in the art who simply reduced the inventor's idea to practice is not necessarily a joint inventor, even if the specification discloses that embodiment to satisfy the best mode requirement.

Furthermore, a co-inventor need not make a contribution to every claim of a patent. See 35 U.S.C. § 116. A contribution to one claim is enough. Thus, the critical question for joint conception is who conceived, as that term is used in the patent law, the subject matter of the claims at issue.

...

A. Claim 33
The district court determined that Choi contributed to the conception of the subject matter of claim 33. Claim 33 (with emphasis to highlight relevant elements) reads:

A surgical instrument for providing communication through an anatomical organ structure, comprising:

- means having an abutment member and shaft longitudinally accommodatable within an outer sleeve, longitudinal movement of said shaft inside said sleeve being limited by contact of said abutment member with said sleeve, said shaft having a distal end with a distal blade surface tapering into a sharp distal point, said distal blade surface being perforated along one side by an aperture, for puncturing an anatomical organ structure when subjected to force along the longitudinal axis of said shaft;

- means having a blunt distal bearing surface, slidably extending through said aperture, for reciprocating through said aperture while said abutment member is in stationary contact with said sleeve;

- means positionable between said puncturing means and said reciprocating means for biasing a distal section of said reciprocating means to protrude beyond said aperture and permitting said distal section of said reciprocating means to recede into said aperture when said bearing surface is subject to force along its axis . . . ; and

- means connectible to the proximal end of said puncturing means for responding to longitudinal movement of said reciprocating means relative to said puncturing means and creating a sensible signal having one state upon recision of said distal section of said reciprocating means into said aperture and another state upon protrusion of said distal section of said reciprocating means from said aperture.

156

To determine whether Choi made a contribution to the conception of the subject matter of claim 33, this court must determine what Choi's contribution was and then whether that contribution's role appears in the claimed invention. If Choi in fact contributed to the invention defined by claim 33, he is a joint inventor of that claim.

Figures 18 and 19 of the '773 patent illustrate an embodiment of claim 33. These figures show a trocar blade with an aperture through which a blunt rod can extend. When the trocar blade penetrates the inner wall of a cavity, a spring releases the rod, which juts out past the end of the trocar blade and prevents the blade from cutting further. The embodiment also includes a structure that gives the surgeon aural and visual signals when the blade nears penetration.

The district court found that Yoon conceived of the use of a blunt probe. However, the court found that Choi conceived of and thereby contributed two features contained in the embodiment shown in figures 18 and 19: first, Choi conceived of locating the blunt probe in the trocar shaft and allowing it to pass through an aperture in the blade surface; second, Choi conceived of the "means . . . for . . . creating a sensible signal."

If Choi did indeed conceive of "locating the blunt probe in the shaft and allowing it to pass through an aperture in the blade surface," he contributed to the subject matter of claim 33. Claim 33 requires that the "distal blade surface" be "perforated along one side by an aperture" and requires the "shaft" to be "longitudinally accommodatable within [the] outer sleeve." Properly construed, claim 33 includes the elements that Choi contributed to the invention according to the district court's findings.

In making this finding, the district court relied extensively on Choi's testimony. Choi testified that the idea of extending the blunt probe through an aperture in the trocar blade itself was his idea. To corroborate this testimony, Choi produced a series of sketches he created while working with Yoon. One sketch shows a probe inside the shaft of a trocar blade, extending through an opening in the side of the end of the blade.

...

In sum, after full consideration of the relevant evidence, the district court determined that Choi conceived part of the invention recited in claim 33. This court detects no cause to reverse this determination.

...

Based on the 1998 Federal Circuit case of *Ethicon Inc. v. U.S. Surgical* Corp., the test for inventorship is whether a person has made an original contribution to the conception of at least one of the claims in the patent application. Conception is "the formation in the mind of the inventor, of a definite and permanent idea of the complete and operative invention...." An invention is complete and operative "only when the idea is so clearly defined in the inventor's mind that only ordinary skill would be necessary to reduce the invention to practice, without extensive research or experimentation." Note that, under the inventorship test, a colleague, a supervisor, an outside expert, a research assistant, or a technician, even though they may gather essential data or construct a prototype of the invention, are not inventors unless they contribute to the conception of the claimed invention.

Contribution to a "claimed invention"

Both patent applications and issued patents typically have more than one inventor and more than one claim. Therefore, patent practitioners could—at the direction of their client—omit certain claims in the patent application to remove the contribution of a particular inventor. This would not only affect the inventorship of the patent application; it could ultimately affect the ownership of the patent application or issued patent, as discussed in the next section.

Who Is the Owner?

Introduction

The inventors named on a patent application are the owners of the patent application (and any subsequent issued patent) unless they transfer their interest to another person or entity. Only the inventors themselves, or those who receive interest from the inventors, can own a patent or patent application. In reality, while an employee generally owns their inventions when they are conceived, this ownership is almost always immediately transferred to their employer. The immediate transfer is based on either: (1) an employment agreement that assigns all inventions from the employee to the employer, or (2) case law that states when the employee is hired to invent a particular invention or solve the particular problem of the invention, then the invention is owned by the employer. See *United States v. Dubilier Condenser Corp.* (1933). Inventors who do not have an obligation to transfer the ownership of their rights continue to be owner of the patent application.

According to the Patent Laws, "In the absence of any agreement to the contrary, each of the joint owners of a patent may make, use, offer to sell, or sell the patented invention ... without the consent of and without accounting to the other owners." (35 U.S.C. 262). Note that *each* of the inventors has *full* rights, which can bend well-established mathematical laws (100% of the patent rights divided by 3 inventors equals 3 inventors each with 100% of the patent rights). While a bizarre result, this is very practical since it is very difficult to split up the rights to an issued patent. To avoid these difficult questions, the patent laws bend mathematical rules and allow *each* of the inventors to have *full* rights. In reality, this forces many inventors to establish ownership rights prior to the filing of a patent application.

Case Law

The following section includes a court decision on ownership issues. This section includes another excerpt from the 1998 Federal Circuit case of *Ethicon Inc. v. U.S. Surgical Corp.* that specifically distinguishes between questions of patent ownership and questions of inventorship.

Ethicon Inc. v. U.S. Surgical Corp. **(Fed. Cir. 1998)**

Circuit Judge Rader for the court:

...

IV. SCOPE OF THE CHOI-U.S. SURGICAL LICENSE

In the context of joint inventorship, each co-inventor presumptively owns a pro rata undivided interest in the entire patent, no matter what their respective contributions. Several provisions of the Patent Act combine to dictate this rule. 35 U.S.C. § 116 states that a joint inventor need not make a contribution "to the subject matter of every claim of the patent." Section 261 continues to provide that "patents shall have the attributes of personal property." This provision suggests that property rights, including ownership, attach to patents as a whole, not individual claims. Moreover, section 262 continues to speak of "joint owners of a patent," not joint owners of a claim. Thus, a joint inventor as to even one claim enjoys a presumption of ownership in the entire patent.

This rule presents the prospect that a co-inventor of only one claim might gain entitlement to ownership of a patent with dozens of claims. As noted, the Patent Act accounts for that occurrence: "Inventors may apply for a patent jointly even though . . . each did not make a contribution to the subject matter of every claim." 35 U.S.C. § 116 (emphasis added). Thus, where inventors choose to cooperate in the inventive process, their joint inventions may become joint property without some express agreement to the contrary. In this case, Yoon must now effectively share with Choi ownership of all the claims, even those which he invented by himself. Thus, Choi had the power to license rights in the entire patent.

...

V. RETROACTIVE LICENSURE

Ethicon argues that even if the license agreement is enforceable as to the entire patent, it should still be allowed to proceed against U.S. Surgical to recover damages for pre-license infringement. This court agrees with Ethicon's challenge to the retroactive effect of Choi's license, but must affirm the dismissal of the case based on Choi's refusal to join as plaintiff in the suit.

...

[T]he grant of a license by one co-owner cannot deprive the other co-owner of the right to sue for accrued damages for past infringement. That would require a release, not a license, and the rights of a patent co-owner, absent agreement to the contrary, do not extend to granting a release that would defeat an action by other co-owners to recover damages for past infringement.

Thus, Choi's "retroactive license" to U.S. Surgical attempts to operate as the combination of a release and a prospective license. Nonetheless Choi cannot release U.S. Surgical from its liability for past accrued damages to Ethicon, only from liability to himself.

As a matter of substantive patent law, all co-owners must ordinarily consent to join as plaintiffs in an infringement suit. Consequently, "one co-owner has the right to impede the other co-owner's ability to sue infringers by refusing to voluntarily join in such a suit."

This rule finds support in section 262 of the Patent Act: "In the absence of any agreement to the contrary, each of the joint owners of a patent may make, use, offer to sell, or sell the patented invention within the United States, or import the patented invention into the United States, without the consent of and without accounting to the other owners." This freedom to exploit the patent without a duty to account to other co-owners also allows co-owners to freely license others to exploit the patent without the consent of other co-owners. Thus, the congressional policy expressed by section 262 is that patent co-owners are "at the mercy of each other."

...

Because Choi did not consent to an infringement suit against U.S. Surgical and indeed can no longer consent due to his grant of an exclusive license with its accompanying "right to sue," Ethicon's complaint lacks the participation of a co-owner of the patent. Accordingly, this court must order dismissal of this suit.

...

Comparison of Assignments and Licenses

Introduction to Assignments

As personal property, a patent may be sold or leased to others, may be mortgaged, and may be bequeathed in a will. The patent laws provide for the transfer of a patent, or of a patent application, by an instrument in writing (known as an "assignment"). An assignment transfers the entire interest in a property from an assignor to an assignee. After the assignment, the assignee becomes the owner of the patent and has the same rights of the original owner.

The assignment of the interest in an issued patent or a patent application should be promptly recorded with the USPTO. According to 35 U.S.C. 261, "An assignment... shall be void as against any subsequent purchaser or mortgagee... unless it is recorded in the Patent and Trademark Office within three months from its date or prior to the date of such subsequent purchase or mortgage."

Introduction to Licenses

The difference between assigning and licensing an invention is similar to the difference between selling and renting a house. In a license arrangement, the ownership of the patent does not change.

Some reasons to license *out* patent rights include: (1) generate revenue, (2) access the manufacturing or distribution channels of another company, (3) access the patent portfolio of another company, (4) access the future inventions or improvements by another company, (5) test a market, (6) avoid waste of a by-product, (7) buy an equity interest in a company, (8) settle a patent dispute, and (9) avoid anti-trust or trade regulation problems. Some reasons to license *in* patent rights include: (1) settle a patent dispute, (2) supplement or replace research and development, (3) eliminate development and hasten response time, (4) establish a defensive legal position, and (5) protect a competitive advantage.

A patent license may be limited by the anti-trust laws and by the concept of patent misuse. The anti-trust laws state that patent owners cannot improperly use their patent leverage to restrain competition in a particular market. The concept of patent misuse states that a patent owner cannot broaden the physical or temporal scope of the patent grant to include, for example, royalty payments after the patent expires or royalty payments even if the patent is held invalid. See *Brulotte v. Thys* (Supreme Court 1964) and *Lear v. Adkins* (Supreme Court 1969), respectively.

In addition to the statutory limitations, a patent license may be voluntarily limited by:

- A time period (e.g., 3 years);
- A geographical location (e.g., only in California);
- Field-of-use (e.g., after-market only); or
- Other provisions (e.g., sold only to certified doctors).

What right is granted in a License?

Patents rights include the right to exclude others from making, using, selling, offering to sell, and importing the subject matter of a claim. Accordingly, a license cannot grant the right to make and sell a product because there is no such patent right. Further, a license cannot grant the right to exclude others to several companies at the same time because the companies themselves would be excluded. So, what rights are included in a patent license? A patent license includes the right *not to be sued* by the patent owner.

Inclusion of "Know-How"

Assignments and licenses for patent rights can also include an assignment or license for trade secrets or "know-how." By including know-how in a patent license, the patent owner may avoid the prohibition against patent misuse. In *Aronson v. Quickpoint* (Supreme Court 1979), the license included a grant of patent rights and know-how for a royalty of 5% if the patent application issued, and of 2.5% if the patent application did not issue within 5 years. No patent was ever issued. After 19 years, the licensee sued to cease payments to the licensor; however, the Court enforced the license because the patent and non-patent royalties were not inextricably intertwined.

About the Author

Jeffrey Schox is a Registered Patent Attorney and the founding member of Schox Patent Group, a boutique patent firm devoted to startup ventures. Drawing on his experience in patent law and angel investing, he builds patent portfolios that enable startups to increase value and attract funding. His clients have attracted investments from high-profile venture capital firms, including Accel, Andreessen Horowitz, Bessemer, Founders Fund, Greylock, Khosla, Kleiner Perkins, Sequoia, and Union Square. With degrees in mechanical and electrical engineering from the University of Michigan, he has filed over 500 patent applications on a broad range of cutting-edge inventions, including vehicle systems, medical devices, electrical systems, computer software, and clean technologies. As a Consulting Professor for Stanford University, Jeffrey teaches the course "Patent Prosecution" in the law school, and the course "Patent Law and Strategy for Innovators and Entrepreneurs" in the engineering school. Jeffrey can be reached via e-mail (JSchox@gmail.com) and followed on Twitter (@JSchox).

Made in the USA
Lexington, KY
14 July 2013